D1311901

INDIANA
UNIVERSITY
SOUTHEAST
LIBRARY

FACTS ON FILE

Wildlife
atlas

Robin Kerrod and John Stidworthy

Culab
QH
84
.K47
1997

Facts On File, Inc.

CONTENTS

ABOUT THIS BOOK

The *Facts On File Wildlife Atlas* is divided into two main sections. The introductory section, pages 4 to 23, describes the different types of wildlife in the world and explains how and why each region has its own unique mix of creatures. In this book, we have used the term wildlife to mean wild plants and animals, not those domesticated or introduced to a region by people. The regional section surveys the wildlife of each continent and its regions in turn. The names of the creatures as they are numbered on the large maps showing plants and animals are listed on pages 79 and 80.

Acknowledgments
Originally produced for George Philip Limited by Lionheart Books, London
Art Editor: Ben White
Project Editor and Photo Research: Lionel Bender
All artwork by Chris Forsey

Executive Editor: Caroline Rayner
Art Editor: Karen Ferguson
Editor: Kara Turner
Cartographic Editors: B. M. Willett, Jenny Allen

Cover photo acknowledgments
Premaphotos Wildlife /W. Lankinen /Aquila top left, /K. G. Preston-Mafham centre bottom left, /R. A. Preston-Mafham centre right

Cartography by Philip's

First published in Great Britain in 1992
by George Philip Limited, an imprint of Reed Books, Michelin House, 81 Fulham Road, London SW3 6RB, and Auckland and Melbourne
Second edition 1997

Text and maps copyright © 1992, 1997 George Philip Limited

First published in the United States of America by Facts On File, Inc.

All rights reserved. No part of this book may be reproduced or utilized in any form or by any means, electronic or mechanical, including photocopying, recording, or by any information storage or retrieval systems, without permission in writing from the publisher. For information contact:

Facts On File, Inc.
11 Penn Plaza
New York, NY 10001

Library of Congress Cataloging-in-Publication Data
Kerrod, Robin.
  [Philip's wildlife atlas]
  Facts On File wildlife atlas / Robin Kerrod and John Stidworthy.
    p. cm.
  Originally published: Philip's wildlife atlas. 1992.
  Includes index.
  Summary: Describes the different types of wildlife in the world and explains how and why each region has its own unique mix of creatures; focuses on habitats, evolution, migratory patterns, and danger of extinction.
  ISBN 0–8160–3714–0
  1. Biogeography—Juvenile literature. 2. Biogeography—Maps—Juvenile literature. 3. Habitat (Ecology)—Juvenile literature. 4. Animals—Juvenile literature. 5. Plants—Juvenile literature. [1. Habitat (Ecology) 2. Animals. 3. Plants. 4. Ecology.]
  I. Stidworthy, John, 1943– . II. Facts On File, Inc.
  QH84.K47 1997
  578' . 09—dc21
                        97–15967

Facts On File books are available at special discounts when purchased in bulk quantities for businesses, associations, institutions or sales promotions. Please call our Special Sales Department in New York at (212) 967–8800 or (800) 322–8755. You can find Facts On File on the World Wide Web at http://www.factsonfile.com

10 9 8 7 6 5 4 3 2 1

Printed in China

LOCATOR MAPS

The first page of each continent chapter has a globe at the top of the page to show the location of the continent within the world. Europe includes Russia west of the Ural Mountains, while Russia east of the Urals is in Asia. There are also small locator maps within the map key boxes. The green areas on these show how the maps fit into their larger regions.

SCALE A map at a scale of "1:35 000 000" means that the real distance on the ground is 35 million times bigger than it is on the map. One inch represents 35 million inches, or 560 miles.

Map scale 1:35 000 000

| 0 | 350km | 700km | 1050km |

| 0 | 350miles | 700miles |

HEIGHT OF THE LAND
In every map key box there is an explanation like this on the different colors and how they show the height of the land. We use shades of green for lowland and brown for highland. The highest land of all is white. The "shadows" give an impression of steep slopes, and a black triangle is the symbol for the top of a mountain with its height in feet.

Kilimanjaro ▲
19 341

	over 18 000 feet
	12 000–18 000
	6 000–12 000
	3 000–6 000
	1 000–3 000
	500–1 000
sea level	0–500 feet
	below sea level

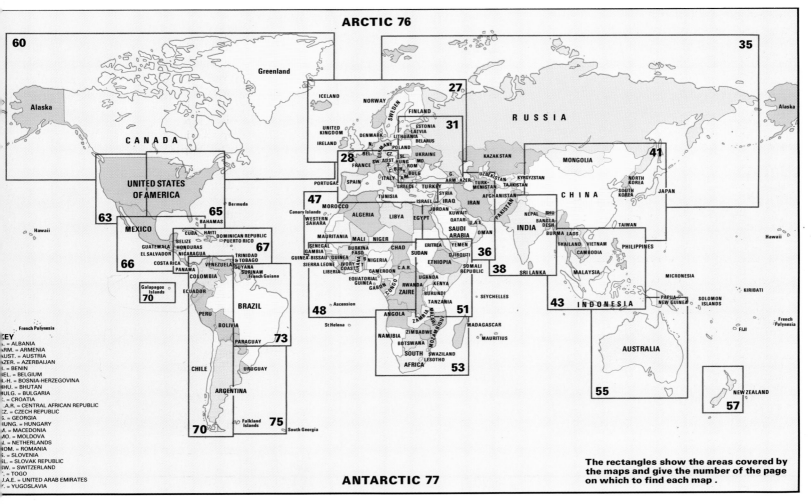

ARCTIC 76

ANTARCTIC 77

KEY
A. = ALBANIA
ARM. = ARMENIA
AUST. = AUSTRIA
AZER. = AZERBAIJAN
B. = BENIN
BEL. = BELGIUM
B.-H. = BOSNIA-HERZEGOVINA
BHU. = BHUTAN
BULG. = BULGARIA
C. = CROATIA
C.A.R. = CENTRAL AFRICAN REPUBLIC
CZ. = CZECH REPUBLIC
G. = GEORGIA
HUNG. = HUNGARY
MA. = MACEDONIA
MO. = MOLDOVA
N. = NETHERLANDS
ROM. = ROMANIA
S. = SLOVENIA
SL. = SLOVAK REPUBLIC
T. = TOGO
SW. = SWITZERLAND
U.A.E. = UNITED ARAB EMIRATES
Y. = YUGOSLAVIA

The rectangles show the areas covered by the maps and give the number of the page on which to find each map.

Animals and Plants

No one knows exactly how many different kinds of animals there are in the world. There may be as many as two million. Over a million kinds are already known and cataloged. Just to write a list of their names would fill more than 80 books the size of this one. Many new animals – especially small ones like beetles – are discovered every year. There are fewer kinds of plants, but there are still hundreds of thousands of them.

FOOD MAKERS AND TAKERS

In one way plants are more important than animals. Without plants no animal would be able to live. Plants trap sunlight and use its energy to make food and so build up the chemicals of which they are made. Animals cannot do this, yet they need food too. They must eat plants or other animals that have fed on plants.

THE FRIENDLY EARTH

Our planet Earth provides the right conditions for plants and animals to live over a large part of its surface. For example, in order to live and grow plants need water. They also need the air around them, especially two of the gases it contains. They breathe oxygen just as animals do, and they need carbon dioxide. From this simple chemical more complicated ones are made in each plant's body.

FUR AND FEATHERS RULE

From the antelopes and ostriches of the Equator, to the arctic foxes and penguins of the polar regions, animals grace the stamps of every country. Birds and mammals can live in so many places because mammals have fur coats, and birds have feathers, that keep them insulated from the world outside.

RELYING ON ONE ANOTHER

Like other animals, we humans rely for o[...] food entirely on the plants and animals th[...] surround us. One difference is that we far[...] many of the things we eat. We grow plan[...] as crops and have bred some for our ow[...] benefit. These plants are now very differe[...] from their wild relatives. It is the same wi[...] farm animals. But, like all living things, we ne[...] to have the right gases in the atmospher[...] the right temperature, and one another.

DIFFERENT PLACES AND FACES

Although much of the Earth can support li[...] conditions vary from place to place. Son[...] parts are hotter than others. Some are ve[...] wet, and some are very dry. There a[...] mountains, valleys and lakes and all produ[...] different kinds of surroundings or habita[...] Different kinds of animals and plants live [...] each habitat. Each particular kind, or speci[...] of living thing is adapted to its environmen[...] That is, it is able to fit into, and survive in[...] particular type of surrounding.

WHY LIVE HERE?

This atlas is about what kinds of animals a[...] plants live where. You can also find out son[...] of the reasons why they live where they d[...] Forest animals are adapted, by their sha[...] and the way they behave, to their fore[...] surroundings. But different forests ha[...] different mixes of species.

CREATURES GREAT AND SMALL

Plant types. The simplest plants are algae such as the green slime that grows on trees. Many algae have just a single cell and are tiny, but some, the seaweeds, in a few cases grow up to 100 feet long. Algae live in water or grow in damp places. The most complex plants are flowering plants, such as the tree aloe (left). They range from low-growing types to huge trees such as oaks and eucalyptus, and are found in a wide range of conditions. Most nonflowering plants, like mosses and ferns, are small and live in warm, damp places, like the ferns (right) growing in Borneo.

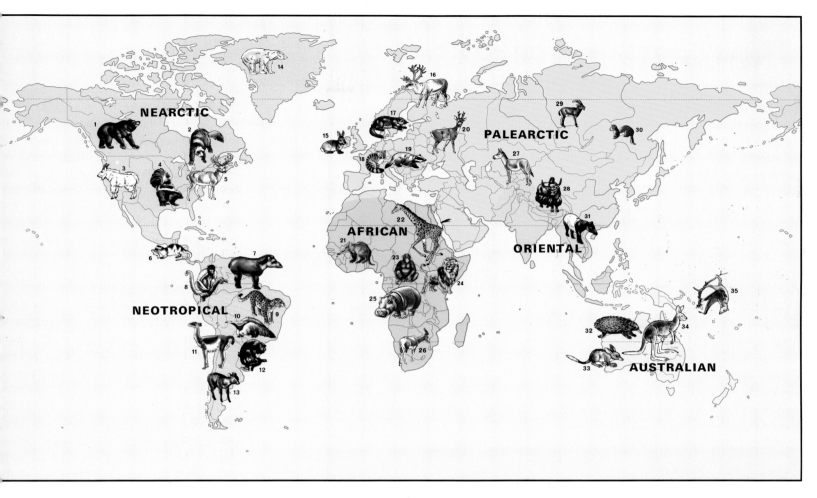

NEARCTIC

PALEARCTIC

AFRICAN

ORIENTAL

NEOTROPICAL

AUSTRALIAN

ZOOGEOGRAPHIC REALMS

1 Grizzly bear	12 Howler monkey	24 Lion
2 Wolverine	13 Pudu	25 Hippopotamus
3 Mountain goat	14 Polar bear	26 Bontebok
4 Striped skunk	15 Mountain hare	27 Asiatic ass
5 White-tailed deer	16 Reindeer	28 Yak
6 Yapok	17 Otter	29 Siberian ibex
7 Tapir	18 Wild cat	30 Kolinsky
8 Humbolt's woolly monkey	19 Eurasian badger	31 Malayan tapir
9 Panther	20 Roe deer	32 Echidna
10 Giant anteater	21 Aardvark	33 Bandicoot
11 Llama	22 Giraffe	34 Kangaroo
	23 Chimpanzee	35 Cuscus

▲ *The zoogeographic regions.*
Each part of the world contains its own mix of animals. Some are found only in that region. Others also live nearby. Animals cannot easily spread to other regions. They are stopped by barriers. Australian animals cannot cross the sea, nor African species the deserts. The Palearctic and Nearctic regions are most alike.

Animal types. Animals range from single-celled creatures like amoeba to complex types like us, with millions of cells. Single-celled animals usually live in water. So do other invertebrates – animals that do not have a backbone. But some, such as snails and earthworms, are found on land. One group, the insects, are the most successful animals on land. They range from flies to odd beetles like the one shown (left). The most complex animals are those we like to think are "best" because we belong among them – the vertebrates, or animals with a backbone. They include large animals, such as the leopard (right).

Natural Habitats

The warmest parts of the Earth are close to the Equator. The further you go from this imaginary line, the colder it is likely to be. Rainfall varies in different places too. In some parts of the world winds carry clouds which give plenty of rain. Other places may not see a cloud from one year to the next. Temperature and rainfall together make an area's climate.

THE TROPICS

Different climates allow different plants to grow. Tropical forest grows where it is hot and wet. Many different plants live here, and trees flourish. Where it is hot, but there is not enough rain for trees, grass may still grow well, giving the type of vegetation known as tropical grassland. Where there is not enough rain even for a cover of grasses, you may find a hot desert with few plants.

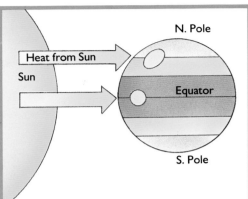

▲ THE SUN'S WARMTH

Sunshine reaching the Earth warms the Equator much more than the polar regions. The same amount of energy has to spread over a greater area toward the poles, where the Earth's surface slopes away from the Sun.

WARM AND DAMP

Not so many kinds of plants grow in the temperate regions away from the tropics but there are still forests where it is wet enough. The trees here may shed their leaves in winter. Further north the trees are more likely to be conifers such as spruces and firs. In drier places, temperate grasslands, such as the steppes of Asia, are the main vegetation.

COLD AND DESOLATE

In the far north and south it is very cold. Plants cannot get much water because the ground is often frozen. Only a few kinds of plant grow in these tundra conditions. They do not grow tall and there are no trees.

ANIMAL LIFE

Each main kind of natural habitat – forest, desert, or grasslands – provides a different type of home for animals and each has developed its own way of life. For instance, many grassland animals can run fast on long legs, and have the right kind of teeth and stomachs for eating grass. But although grasslands in different regions of the world look alike, the plants that grow may belong to different species. The animals, too, may act in similar ways, but may not be closely related. For example, some Australian kangaroos behave like African antelopes.

◄ *African elephants cluster around a waterhole. Elephants need a hot climate, enough water to drink, and a good supply of plants to eat all year.*

THE LAND'S SHARE
About two-thirds of the Earth is covered by sea. Just one-third is land. Of this:
- Desert covers over 15 percent.
- Tropical forest covers 15 percent.
- Temperate forest covers over 20 percent.
- Grasslands cover over 15 percent.
- Mountain and tundra vegetation cover 5 percent

The rest is mostly semidesert.

WORLD HABITATS

The map shows the main habitat in each area. The sketches show a typical animal from each habitat. The type of habitat in an area depends roughly on how far it is from the equator. But even near the equator, on high mountains it can be cold. There, only plants like those in the tundra near the poles grow.

Polar desert

Tundra and mountain

Temperate forest

Mediterranean

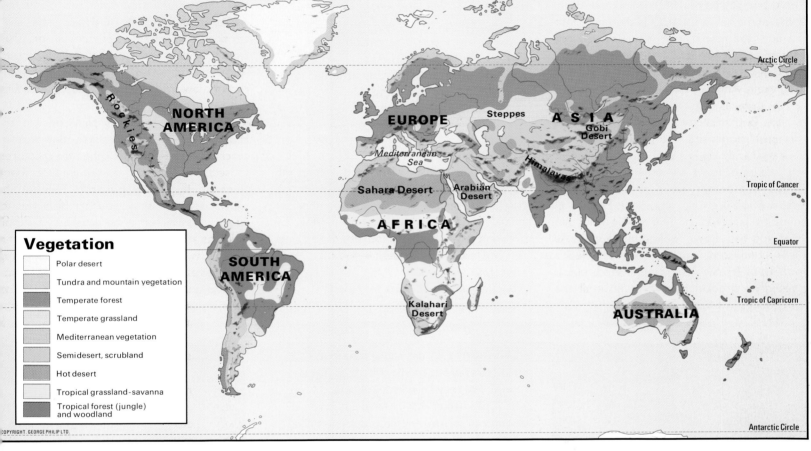

ARCTIC CIRCLE

NORTH AMERICA

Rockies

EUROPE

Steppes

ASIA

Gobi Desert

Mediterranean Sea

Himalayas

Tropic of Cancer

Sahara Desert

Arabian Desert

AFRICA

Equator

SOUTH AMERICA

Kalahari Desert

Tropic of Capricorn

AUSTRALIA

Antarctic Circle

Vegetation

- Polar desert
- Tundra and mountain vegetation
- Temperate forest
- Temperate grassland
- Mediterranean vegetation
- Semidesert, scrubland
- Hot desert
- Tropical grassland-savanna
- Tropical forest (jungle) and woodland

COPYRIGHT. GEORGE PHILIP LTD.

Temperate grassland

Semidesert

Hot desert

Tropical grassland

Tropical forest

Webs of Life

Grass growing on an African plain is eaten by a zebra. The grass has trapped the Sun's energy and used it to live and to grow new leaves. The zebra that eats the grass now has some of the energy that came from the Sun. Some of this energy is stored in its body. But it uses the rest for moving and keeping itself warm. This energy is lost from its body.

LINKED TOGETHER

The zebra may be caught by a lion and eaten. Some of the zebra's energy is then built into the lion, the rest is lost. Most living things pass on energy like this. The grass, the zebra and the lion are all links in what is called a food chain. Another example of a food chain is: acacia leaves eaten by giraffe; giraffe eaten by lion. But these two examples are linked too. Both chains end with the lion.

Very rarely do we find food chains that are separate from all others. The same animal can belong in many food chains. Suppose you drew out all the food chains an animal is involved in. You would find that what you had drawn looked like a web. All these connected food chains are called a food web. It may look complicated, but it gives quite a good picture of how all the living things in a habitat are linked.

PYRAMID OF NUMBERS

There are always fewer meat-eaters than plant-eaters. This is because:
1. Only some of the energy in food is passed on at each stage along a food chain.
2. Most meat-eaters are bigger than the things they eat.
3. If there were more meat-eaters they would run out of food to hunt.

So in a wood you might find:
- 1 fox hunting among
- 50 pheasants hunting among
- 3,000 worms eating
- 100,000 leaves.

BREAKING DOWN

If the bodies of dead plants and animals did not rot away, the world would soon be clogged with them. A large number of animals and fungi make their living by breaking down, or decomposing, dead plants and animals. Decomposers include:
- worms
- beetles and tiny insects in the soil
- microscopic bacteria.

NATURE'S RECYCLING

Decomposers use the energy locked up in dead bodies and break down the bodies into smaller pieces and eventually into simple chemicals. These simple chemicals can be recycled, and, once more, living things build them into their bodies.

WEBS IN THE SEA

There are food chains and webs in the sea too. The most important sea plants are microscopic ones floating near the sea's surface. They are called phytoplankton. They trap the Sun's energy and produce oxygen just like land plants. There are so many in the vast oceans that they make two-thirds of the world's oxygen.

Feeding on the phytoplankton are the zooplankton. Some of these tiny floating animals are the young of other sea creatures. Others, including shrimp-like animals, spend all their lives in the plankton. Fish eat the plankton. In turn they are eaten by larger fish and squid, which may be caught by seals or dolphins at the top of the chain.

There are decomposers in the sea too, helping to break down dead bodies. Crabs and many smaller sea animals sift scraps of dead matter from the water.

PLANT-EATERS are eating food that is often plentiful, but can be difficult to digest. A single leaf may have little useful food in it. A plant-eater may need to eat large amounts to survive. Anyone who has watched a caterpillar chomping leaves or a horse eating grass will know what big amounts they get through. Plant-eaters may spend a large part of their day feeding.

Plants can be tough to eat. An insect like the alpine grasshopper (left) has strong chewing jaws. So does the bontebok (right). This antelope has large teeth in the side of its mouth to grind the food, and a large gut to put it in while it is digested.

Where plants grow well, plant-eaters can live in huge numbers, whether they are hordes of insects in Scandinavia or large herds of zebra in Africa.

Decomposers

A simple food chain in action.
Light energy from the Sun is trapped by plants. Rabbits feed on the plants, taking some of their energy. The fox feeds on the rabbits, and is the top link in this chain. More hidden from view are the actions of decomposers like fungi (above). These break down the dead leaves that fall to the ground. Others, like the beetle (below), help in this. Animal bodies, like dead plants, are broken down by decomposers.

Decomposers

Sun

Plants

Plant-eaters

Meat-eaters

MEAT-EATERS need to search for their prey – the animals they hunt. They need sharp senses to find them, and weapons to kill them. These weapons are often sharp claws and teeth, as in the lace monitor (left), but they can also be stings, as in wasps, or venomous bites, as in spiders.

Although animals may be difficult to catch and kill, their meat is full of useful food. Anteaters have to shovel in large numbers of tiny prey, but most meat-eaters get their food in larger lumps. They can afford to spend time resting between meals. A lion spends more time asleep than awake. Some animals feed on carrion – animals that are already dead. Vultures like those (right) feeding on a carcass left by a lion are meat-eaters, but they are also the first of many decomposers.

Grassland Life

Large areas of grassland occur in the dry middle of most continents, where rain comes for just part of the year. In temperate regions the grass is short. The grassland has different names according to which country it is in. In North America the grasslands are called prairies. Nowadays they are mostly farmed rather than wild.

In eastern Europe and northern Asia the grasslands are called steppes. Temperate grasslands also grow in Australia and South America (the pampas). Mediterranean-type scrub (grass with low woody shrubs) grows in places where summers are hot and dry and winters are cool and wet.

HOT GRASSLANDS

Tropical grassland, called savanna, is found over a large area of Africa. There is a big area in South America too, and smaller areas in northern Australia and India.

HERDS

On open grassland, animals can see a long way. Plant-eaters need good eyesight to watch out for hunters and move away from them. There are few places to hide, but there is safety in numbers. With more pairs of eyes to look out for trouble, a hunter may think twice before attacking a group of animals together. Many grassland animals, like wildebeest, live in big herds.

SPEED

Speed is useful on the plains to escape enemies. Plant-eaters such as zebra and antelopes run fast on long legs. So do some grassland birds, such as ostriches and emus. Many grassland animals can run at up to 40 miles an hour, but even speeds like this are not always enough to escape grassland hunters. A cheetah can run at 55 miles an hour for a short while.

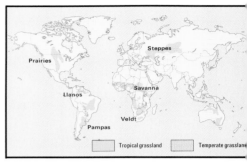

▶ *Wild buffalo* feed on lush grass near a wallow in the Indian grasslands. Indian rhinos are found in the same area, and antelope and deer also graze here. The meat-eaters include jackals and mongooses. The largest one is the tiger. The mix of animals is like that on the African savanna, but the species are different.

▼ *Circling the Serengeti.* The map (left) shows the Serengeti Plain in East Africa. Each year, huge herds of wildebeest move around this area looking for food. At calving time they come here, a place where rain has made the grass grow well for the young to feed. Also on the Serengeti live: springbok and impala antelopes, which eat grass; dik-dik, black rhinos, elephants and giraffes, which feed at different levels in bushes and trees.

Giraffe

African elephant

Springbok

Kudu

Black rhino

Dikdik

SHARING

On some grasslands many different animal species "share" the food. They can do this because they feed in different ways. On the African savanna common zebras eat long grass. Wildebeest graze shorter grass, while the small Thomson's gazelles feed on the short grass others leave behind. The gerenuk, a long-necked antelope, feeds from twigs of bushes. Giraffes browse on taller bushes and trees. By sticking to their own favorite foods, the species do not compete with each other for the same thing.

UNDERGROUND

Grasses have well-developed roots that help them to survive being eaten or burned. Much grassland life goes on below the ground. Rodents burrow in the soil. Some just use burrows to sleep or hide from enemies, but in the steppes and prairies they need them to survive the cold winters. Some rodents, such as mole rats, spend their whole lives in underground tunnels, feeding on the roots they find there.

NORTH AMERICAN GRASSLANDS

The most important animals of the American prairies used to be the bison and the pronghorn (below). Both roamed in herds of many millions, which were always on the move across the plains, keeping the grass short and preventing trees from growing. That was before this area was settled by farmers and the herds were hunted almost to extinction.

Smaller plant-eaters of the prairies include ground squirrels, such as marmots and prairie dogs. These make "towns" of burrow systems with raised entrance mounds. Guard prairie dogs keep watch for the whole community. They need to. Their enemies include hawks and the coyote (below), a smaller relative of the wolf. American badgers also live in this open country. Few trees grow on the prairie, but the Joshua tree (left) can survive in the dry grasslands.

Forest Life

Forest is the natural vegetation of much of the world. There are several kinds:
- Conifer forest – found where the winters are cold and snowy. The trees are mainly evergreens with needle-like leaves.
- Temperate deciduous forest – found where the summers are warm and the winters cool. Most of the trees have broad leaves which are deciduous (shed in fall).
- Tropical forest – found where conditions are hot all year and often very wet. The trees are always growing, always green.

Both conifer forests and temperate deciduous forests are shown as temperate forest on the map.

FOREST FIGURES
- About half the trees growing in the world are in tropical forests.
- Every second of every day an area of the size of a football field is cut down.
- In the temperate forest, an oak tree can be home to more than 300 species of animals and have up to 50,000 caterpillars feeding on it.
- Many animals in temperate forests store food for winter. Squirrels and woodpeckers, for example, store acorns.
- Birds such as warblers migrate to northern woodlands for summer to feed on the many insects.

▼ LIFE IN A CONIFEROUS FOREST.
Birds such as the crossbill are specially adapted for feeding on buds and seeds of spruce. Siberian jays, woodpeckers and nutcrackers can break open cones. The capercaillie feeds on seeds on the ground. Voles and lemmings are among the small plant-eating mammals. Deer, including elk, the largest of all, browse in the forest and nearby swamps. Meat-eaters includ brown bears and the powerful wolverine, both of which can catch deer. Members of the weasel family that have thick fur coats, such as the stoat (ermine) and sable, hunt through the forest in winter. Martens pursue squirrels through the trees. Some animals hibernate or go south for winter.

Woodpecker
Snowy owl
Bear
Stoat
Raven
Wild boar

NORTHERN EVERGREEN
Conifer forest grows in a huge belt across northern parts of America, Europe, and Asia. In the southern hemisphere there is little land in the cool latitudes, but some places, such as New Zealand, have conifer forests.

Big areas of conifer forest may be covered by the same kind of tree – fir or pine, for example. Little grows among the dead needles, and the soil contains few worms and insects. The forest has only a few animal species because food is limited. Conifers provide seeds and bark for the plant-eaters, which in turn are eaten by meat-eaters such as pine martens.

Tropical forest   Temperate forest

FALLING LEAVES
Temperate deciduous forest also grow mainly in North America, Europe and Asi south of the great coniferous forests. Th trees shed their leaves in the fall and grow new ones in the spring. This gives a chanc for many ground plants to grow and flowe in spring before the trees are in leaf. Even summer enough light filters through th trees for undergrowth to grow.

Old leaves rot away quite fast, supportin many decomposers in the soil beneath an making the soil fertile. Many more kind of animals and plants are at home in th deciduous forests than in conifer forests.

WOODLAND VARIETY

In the temperate forests leaves are eaten by animals such as moth caterpillars. Deer eat leaves and young shoots. Squirrels eat buds and nuts. Mice feed on seeds. There is plenty of food through much of the year, and plenty of plant-eaters for weasels, foxes and sparrowhawks to hunt.

TROPICAL MIX

The greatest variety of life is found in the tropical rain forests. These forests:
  are always hot – the temperature is above 68°F all year;
  are very wet – there is between 100 and 400 inches of rain each year;
  have no seasons – it is always like summer;
  have more species of animal and plant than any other habitat on Earth;
  have very thin soils – leaves and other dead material rot quickly and are used again immediately by other living things;
  have grown for millions of years.

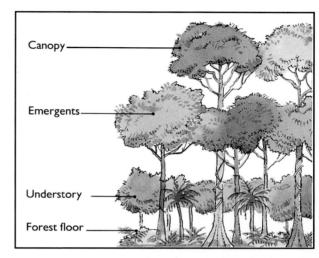

▼ *Canopy to floor.* A few trees in tropical forests stick out above their neighbors. But most of the treetops form a continuous canopy, a thick tangle of leaves and branches. Other plants grow on their branches. If there is enough light, another layer of trees and bushes may grow under the canopy. The dark forest floor is covered with decaying leaves.

Canopy

Emergents

Understory

Forest floor

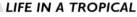

▲ *LIFE IN A TROPICAL FOREST.* The Rusa deer (above top) feeds in a glade in a Javan forest. The crab-eating macaque nearby also feeds on the ground and in the water, but finds leaves, fruit and insects in the trees too. The red-eyed tree frog (above middle) lives in Central America. Frogs like warm, wet conditions and are found in all tropical forests. Some lay their eggs in tiny pools among leaves.

The spectacular weevil (above left) is a plant-eating insect from the New Guinea jungle. Huge spiders like the Malaysian tarantula (above right) catch large insects and even small mice and birds. This one has a burrow on the forest floor. The coati (left) lives in South and Central America. Small groups of them hunt in the trees and on the ground, catching insects, lizards, and other small animals.

Desert and Mountain Life

Deserts have less than 12 inches of rain each year. Some have no rain for several years. Not all are sandy. Some have surfaces of rocks or pebbles. Where it rains a little more, bushes may grow, making it semi-desert or scrub.

Deserts such as the Sahara in North Africa are hot in the daytime for the whole year. The air can be hotter than our bodies and the ground too hot to touch. But even here it may freeze at night under the clear skies. In the deserts of Central Asia it is hot in summer but very cold in winter.

DESERT DODGES

Deserts are difficult places in which to live, but some animals and plants still manage. Desert plants such as cacti have spines for leaves that stop animals from eating them. They make food in their green stems instead of their leaves and store water in them too. They, and other fleshy desert plants, have skins that let little water escape. Desert plants such as salt bush have roots that grow 65 feet deep to tap underground water supplies. Others rely on the brief rains. In some deserts, plants trap nighttime dew for a water supply.

To avoid the heat, many small desert animals are active at night. The burning Sun has little effect 25 inches under the ground, so lizards, snakes, jerboas, and desert foxes hide underground in the day and come out at night.

Some insects and reptiles are good at living in deserts as their skin lets out little water. They turn body waste into a solid paste, not liquid urine, and so save water that way too. The jerboa's nose cools the air it breathes out, so less water is lost in the breath. Jackrabbits have large ears that work like ducts drawing out the heat from the body. Pale colors help reflect sunlight and are good camouflage.

▲ **DESERT LIFE** in the Namib Desert in southern Africa. A ground squirrel (above) makes a brief excursion into the hot Sun. Notice how it is using its tail to shade its body from the Sun. The venomous horned adder (right) is well camouflaged in desert surroundings. The welwitschia (above right) is a strange plant that can live up to a thousand years. Its two long strap-like leaves are good at sucking in the dew that forms on them. Water is stored in a turnip-shaped root.

► **MOUNTAIN LIFE.** The mountain viscacha (right) is at home among the rocky outcrops that dot the grassy slopes high up the Andes Mountains in South America. They live in colonies of up to 70 animals. Guards whistle to alert other viscachas to danger. The Apollo butterfly (above right) lives in the meadows high in the European Alps. The Andean flicker (far right) is a type of woodpecker living in grassland 14,000 feet above sea level.

► MOUNTAIN ZONES

In many ways the change in climate as you go up a mountain is like the change as you go from the Earth's Equator to the poles. You can even see the same belts of vegetation. But their level on any mountain depends on its distance from the Equator. For instance the tree line – above which it is too cold for trees to grow – is:
• up to 13,000 feet at the Equator;
• only 2,000 feet in southern Norway.

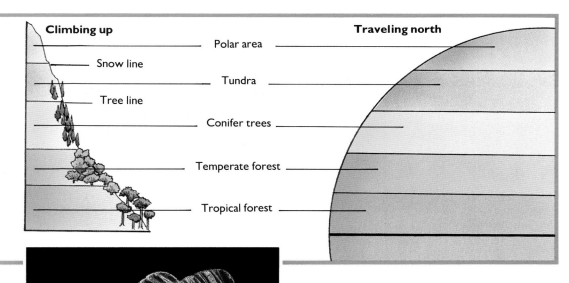

Climbing up | **Traveling north**
Polar area
Snow line
Tundra
Tree line
Conifer trees
Temperate forest
Tropical forest

OLAR DESERTS

ear the poles are deserts of ice and snow. is too bitterly cold for plants to live here, it is too cold for most animals. But some ds and mammals survive here, getting od from the seas that surround the . Penguins have a thick layer of fat under e skin, which protects them from the ld water and the freezing air. They live in uthern polar regions. Polar bears have enty of fat too and a thick fur coat to keep em warm. They live in the arctic.

On the tundra near the poles the winters e bleak, but the summer days are long. In mmer, plants grow well, and hardy tundra imals are joined by migratory birds.

ISLANDS ON THE LAND

Mountains sticking up from the surrounding lowlands are like islands. Their climate differs from the lowlands, and their wildlife may be quite different too.

As you climb a mountain it becomes colder. A high mountain may be capped with snow and ice, even if it is on the Equator, like Kilimanjaro in Africa. On many mountains, animal and plant life changes dramatically between the lower slopes and the mountain tops (see above). Animals such as ibex, the alpaca, and the yak are found only in mountain regions. For lowland animals like mongooses and zebra, mountains are a barrier they cannot cross.

Life in Water

The sea is vast. Most of the ocean is about 3 miles deep, but around the edge there is a "shelf" where it is only 650 feet deep. Then the sea floor plunges down. On the sea bed are huge valleys and mountains. Most of this world is very dark. Sunlight does not penetrate much below the sea surface, so this is where the plants are found.

Animals are most common near the sea surface too, but some live down in the black depths. They have to rely on food falling from above. Crabs and their relatives scavenge on the sea bottom. Strange fish, some with their own lights, make the most of the occasional passing meal.

A SALTY HOME

Many kinds of animals live in the sea. Primitive animals like jellyfish and sponges have been living there for hundreds of millions of years. The shelled animals, or mollusks, are common, and there are many different types of worms. Lobsters, starfish, backboned animals such as fish and whales, all share the sea.

Most of the sea forms one large habitat although sea temperatures and warm and cold currents can affect life locally. Tropical coral reefs have an amazing variety of life. Estuaries, where rivers meet the sea, are often particularly rich in species.

SEA FACTS

The sea contains:
- The deepest "valleys" in the world. Some are 7 miles deep, deeper than the tallest mountain, Everest, is high.
- The biggest animal on Earth, the blue whale – up to 175 tons.
- The biggest animal without a backbone, the giant squid, which can be up to 65 feet long.
- A deep-sea anglerfish in which the female can be 20,000 times bigger than the male, which lives attached to her like a parasite.
- A fish, the ling, that lays up to 28 million eggs. Only two eggs are likely to survive to become adults.

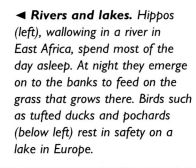

◄ *Rivers and lakes. Hippos (left), wallowing in a river in East Africa, spend most of the day asleep. At night they emerge on to the banks to feed on the grass that grows there. Birds such as tufted ducks and pochards (below left) rest in safety on a lake in Europe.*

▼ *Sea creatures. Bottle-nosed dolphins are at home in the ocean. They hunt fish. Although they are mammals, and the baby swimming below with its mother will feed on milk, they have a streamline, fish-like shape. It is a good design for moving fast through water.*

POND LIFE. *Around a pond there is a gradual change from dry land plants to those such as reeds and kingcups that can grow with their roots in water, and true pondweeds that grow underwater. There are also planktonic algae in the water.*

Tiny shelled animals such as cyclops feed on the plants. Insects like pond skaters are found on the surface. Other insects such as diving beetles and dragonfly larvae live underwater, catching prey. Snails rasp away at water plants with their rough tongues.

Even the smallest pond is likely to contain sticklebacks. Larger ponds may have bigger fish like sunfish, and the fierce pike. Where it is warm enough terrapins hunt too.

FRESHWATERS

Freshwaters include tiny ponds, large lakes, mountain streams, and mighty slow-moving rivers. All provide their own special conditions for life.

Just as in the sea, planktonic plants (see page 8) can be important in freshwater. At some times of the year stagnant water can be so full of them that it looks green. Flowering plants grow in freshwater too. Most root on the bottom, but many, like waterlilies, send leaves and flowers up to the surface.

ANIMALS IN FRESHWATER

Planktonic animals such as water fleas eat the plant plankton. They are fed on by other animals, including fish. Snails, worms, leeches, and a number of insects make freshwater their home. Birds, from herons to swans, feed in water, as do mammals such as otters. Even reptiles, for example terrapins and crocodiles, are adapted for hunting in water.

FRESHWATER FACTS

- Less than 1 percent of all the water in the world is freshwater in lakes, rivers and ponds. Some is locked up as ice.
- The largest body of freshwater is Lake Superior in North America. It covers 32,000 square miles.
- Most lakes are very shallow compared to the sea. The deepest is Lake Baykal in Russia, and it is only 5,250 feet deep.
- Loch Ness, in Scotland, is deeper than the North Sea. Plenty of room for a monster to hide?
- The biggest freshwater fish, the arapaima of South America, can grow up to 15 feet long.
- Frogs, toads and newts are amphibians, which as young live in freshwater and as adults spend much time on land.

Rushes

Reeds

Kingfisher

Dragonfly

Heron

Frog

Coot

Pondweeds

Moorhen

Diving beetle

Arrowhead plant

Newt

Pike

Stickleback

Caddisfly larva

Snail

Evolution

Rocks billions of years old have remains of simple plants in them. We know that by about 650 million years ago there were simple animals like jellyfish. All the earliest animals had soft bodies with no shells or bones so little of them remains.

Later rocks contain hard-skinned animals like trilobites and sea scorpions. Later still we begin to find fossils of animals with backbones. The earliest ones were fish, followed by amphibians, then reptiles. Birds and mammals were the last to appear in the fossil record. We can see that life has changed over this long period. The process of change is called evolution.

COMING AND GOING

As time went on, the plants and animals became "better" and their bodies more complicated. Some of the old kinds managed to survive, but others were squeezed out by new types. Ferns, for instance, were once more common than they are now.

Some living things have disappeared completely. The ammonites, shelled distant relatives of squid, were common in the sea for millions of years. Now they are extinct. The dinosaurs ruled the world for an immense time. They too have gone. Life is competitive. Only animals and plants that fit in well with their surroundings survive.

FAMOUS FOSSILS
• Dinosaurs ruled the Earth for about 135 million years, until 65 million years ago.
• Remains of dinosaurs have been found on all continents except Antarctica.
  "Living fossils" are species surviving when all their relatives are extinct. Some examples to look up:
• The coelacanth, a fish from deep in the Indian Ocean.
• The ginkgo, a tree that survived in China. It is now planted in many towns. Have you seen one?
• The tuatara, a reptile that lives on a few islands near New Zealand.

180 million years ago

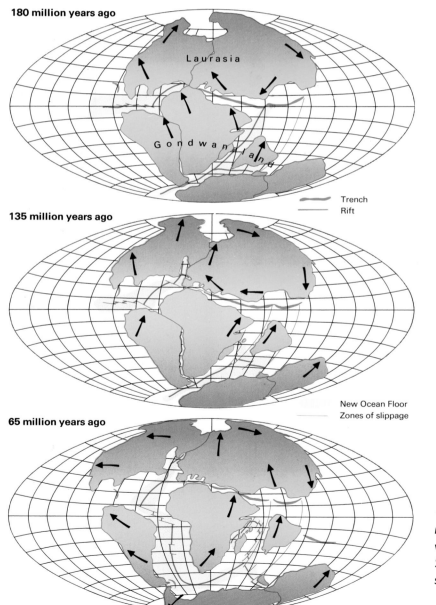

Laurasia

Gondwanaland

〰️ Trench
— Rift

135 million years ago

New Ocean Floor
Zones of slippage

65 million years ago

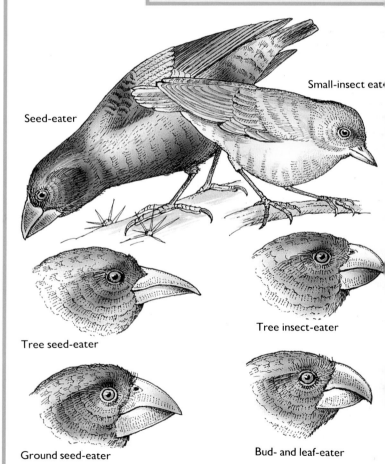

Seed-eater

Small-insect eat

Tree seed-eater

Tree insect-eater

Ground seed-eater

Bud- and leaf-eater

◄ **Moving continents.** 200 million years ago most of the world's land was joined together. Since then blocks of land have split from the main mass and slowly moved across the Earth. Some have joined in new ways, India to Asia, South America to North America. This is partly why animals live where they do.

THE PROCESS OF EVOLUTION

The fossil history of animals shows that amphibians evolved from fish, and birds and mammals from reptiles. We even find "in-between" types, such as the echidna of Australia, which is difficult to call either a reptile or mammal.

The English scientist Charles Darwin explained how he thought this happens. He saw that those animals best fitted to their surroundings do well. After a few generations, all the animals might be the "improved" model. Other, older types would have died out.

Sometimes, of course, conditions, such as the climate, or the plants and animals around may change. A new design may be best now. A new species may then evolve to take advantage of the new situation.

DARWIN'S FINCHES. The naturalist Charles Darwin (below) was the first person to give a good explanation of how and why animals and plants evolve. When a young man, he went on a voyage around the world. He saw many things that he thought about for many years before putting forward his "theory of evolution by natural selection" in 1859.

One place he visited was the Galapagos Islands in the Pacific. Many small finches lived there. Darwin noticed that these animals came in many types (left). For example, there were species with beaks adapted for feeding on seeds, or insects, or buds and fruits. Apart from their beaks they looked rather similar. Darwin guessed that the islands had been colonized by a few birds from the mainland of South America. Once in the Galapagos their descendants had evolved to suit the many possible ways of life.

▲ *African wild dog.* Most African wild dogs look alike. But domestic dogs have been changed by being selectively bred by humans. From the same ancestor (the wolf), we have bred types as different as Alsatians and Pekingese.

▼ *A sunbird looks for a meal.* Sunbirds have long bills to probe flowers for nectar. All birds have beaks that "fit" the food they eat. The theory of natural selection says that those best adapted survive, while the poorly adapted die out.

▼ *Halfway house?* The echidna (below right) is a mammal that lays eggs, but feeds its babies on milk when they hatch. It has fur and is warm-blooded.

▼ *Harlequin frog.* The colors of many animals help them hide from predators, but some have bright colors that attract mates or show that they are dangerous if attacked. This one has a very poisonous skin.

THE SPREAD OF NEW ANIMALS

How the continents are arranged affects how far new kinds of animals and plants can spread. Some "old-fashioned" animals have survived only where they have been cut off from their more "advanced" competitors. Mammals that lay eggs, for example, are only found in the Australian region.

Pouched mammals, such as kangaroos and possums, have survived only in Australia and South America. Both of these continents were islands for most of the last 65 million years when the other modern mammals evolved.

Small islands are often good places to see the results of evolution. Many have birds that cannot fly or are very tame because they have no enemies to threaten them.

Migration

Many animals live in two different parts of the world at different times of the year. Regular journeys made with the seasons are known as migrations. Some of these journeys are quite short. A frog or toad may travel only 500 feet to a pond in spring. Other animals migrate thousands of miles. They do so:

1. To find food.
2. To find the right place to breed.
3. To avoid bad weather.
4. To find a good place to hibernate.

EMIGRATION
Several animals' homes become very overcrowded. Lemmings, locusts, and waxwings can build up such huge colonies that no food is left in their home area. They set off on a one-way journey to find a new place to live.

FEEDING AND BREEDING
Wildebeest, zebras and elephants in some parts of Africa move to find supplies of new grass. In the dry season they scour the land for food and move to where rain is falling.

Whales such as the blue whale swim thousands of miles to breed in warmer water. Turtles migrate to the right sort of sandy beach to lay their eggs. Fur seals swim long distances to special breeding beaches. Birds such as albatrosses, which spend most of their lives at sea, migrate back to their nesting islands.

▶ *Butterflies on migration. Here some brown-veined white butterflies pause in migration across the desert and congregate around a damp patch to find a drink. A number of butterflies make long-distance migrations.*

◀ *ROUTES TO THE SUN. North American birds that migrate south for the winter keep to a small number of major flyways. They follow big geographical features such as the Mississippi River valley or the Pacific coast. Many birds dislike crossing wide stretches of water, so many travel down through Central America. But others take a shorter route by island-hopping across the Caribbean Sea.*

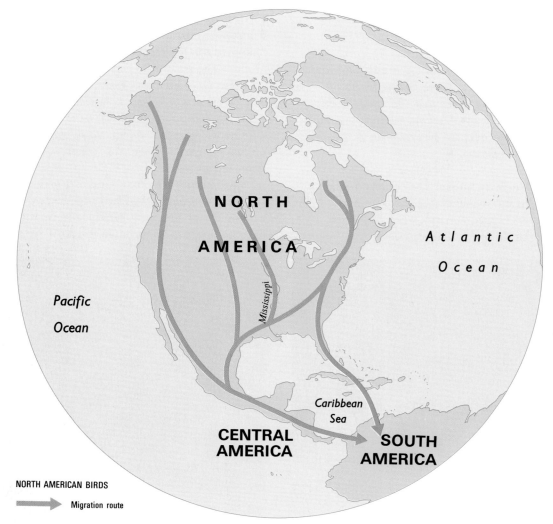

NORTH AMERICAN BIRDS
➡ Migration route

CHAMPION MIGRATORS
- Green turtle – 1,200 miles from Ascension Island to Brazil.
- Grey whale – 12,000 miles from the Arctic to California.
- Caribou – over 500 miles south from the Canadian tundra for winter.
- Monarch butterfly – 1,200 miles from the Great Lakes in the United States to Mexico.
- Desert locust – 3,000 miles from Arabia to West Africa.
- Short-tailed shearwater – 20,000 miles around the Pacific.
- Arctic tern – 22,000 milles from the Arctic to Antarctic.
- Little brown bat – 200 miles.

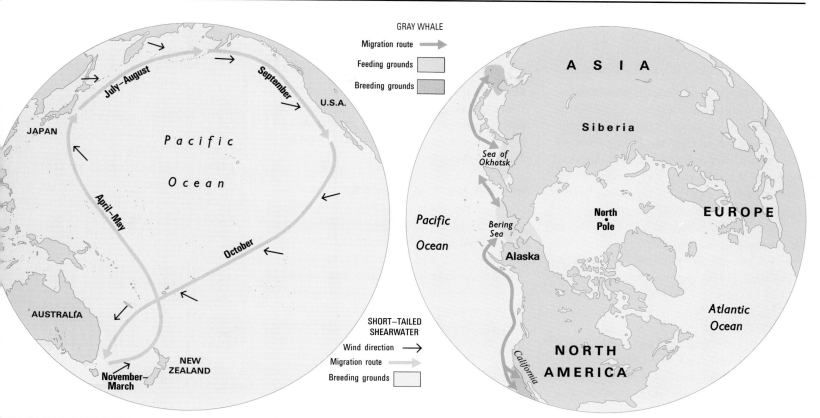

GRAY WHALE
Migration route
Feeding grounds
Breeding grounds

SHORT—TAILED
SHEARWATER
Wind direction
Migration route
Breeding grounds

VOIDING WINTER

any insect-eating birds, such as swifts and
vallows, leave cold countries in fall where
ere is not enough food for them to survive
e winter and keep warm.

Other animals avoid the worst of winter
o. Caribou feed during the summer months
the tundra of the far north. But in the fall
ey travel south to the edge of the forest belt,
here they can find some shelter.

Some bats roost happily in hollow trees
other crannies in the summer but need
e constant conditions of caves to sleep
rough the winter. Little brown bats in
merica sometimes migrate a long way to
d a good cave for hibernation.

YSTERIOUS STEERING

here is much we do not know about how
imals find their way on migration. Birds
ay use the position of stars, the Sun and
ndmarks as guides and other means too.
oung cuckoos have never seen their
rents yet are able to migrate from Europe
Africa and back just as their parents do.

The blue wildebeest provide one of
e world's great spectacles when hundreds
thousands of them migrate. Herds carry
across wide rivers even though many
imals are swept away.

▲ **Circular tour.** The short-tailed
shearwater breeds in the summer (from
November to March) on islands off the south
coast of Australia. It spends the rest of the
year on a huge migration around the Pacific
Ocean, which it covers in a lopsided figure
of eight. As it travels it uses the winds to help
it along. It reaches each area at the best time
of year to find food, returning to its nesting
grounds in time for the next breeding season.

▲ **Gray whales** make one of the longest
mammal migrations. They spend the summer
feeding in cold seas between Alaska and
Siberia. These freeze over in late fall and
the whales move south. They keep moving
until they reach shallow lagoons off the
Californian coast. This is where the whale
calves are born. When the young are strong
enough, they swim north again, covering up
to 50 miles a day.

Wildlife in Danger

It is a sad fact that more kinds of wildlife are in danger today than at any other time before. Species now in danger include not only well-known animals like the giant panda, but also many plants and small animals. Some of those in danger, such as insects of the tropical forests, may become extinct before they have even been "discovered."

Nearly all the problems facing wildlife can be summed up in one word – people. We may kill animals on purpose. We may do things that we never thought would harm wildlife but end up killing it.

HUNTING

If animals are hunted and killed faster than they can breed, they disappear. The American bison was almost hunted to extinction, but it was saved just in time. Tigers and other big cats have been hunted for their fine skins, elephants for their ivory. Even when hunting is illegal, if there is money to be made some people still poach.

Commercial fishing is a kind of hunting too. In some places it has virtually wiped out stocks of fish that were once common.

DESTROYING HABITATS

Perhaps the biggest threat of all to wildlife is the destruction of the wild places of the world. A habitat may be destroyed on purpose, as when a forest is cut down to grow crops. Like Humpty-Dumpty, a broken habitat cannot be restored to the way it was.

Quite often people change habitats by mistake. Some Mediterranean lands had much more vegetation until people let goats roam. Goats feed on leaves from trees. Dry country can be turned into desert by grazing cattle. Chemicals released freely into the countryside can cause all kinds of problems, polluting the air, ground, and water.

Chemicals from power-plant chimneys cause acid rain. This may fall a long way away, where it gradually kills trees.

▶ *The chimpanzee, like other great apes, is an endangered species. Many have been caught in the past for zoos and laboratories. Also, there are few really wild forests left for chimpanzees to live in now.*

SHRINKING WORLD

There is less and less space for animals. Not only do wild places disappear, but farms and fences may stop the movement of animals between those that remain.

REPAIRING THE DAMAGE

Some of the most endangered animals and plants can be saved by breeding in captivity. Most of the best zoos and wildlife parks join together in breeding endangered species. But this can only be an answer for a few.

Most kinds of animals and plants will only be preserved if we set aside areas where they can live without too much interference from people.

SUCCESS AND FAILURE

Animals that have survived by being bred in captivity include:

- The nene, or Hawaiian goose, once down to about 35 individuals, but now back in the hundreds.
- The Arabian oryx, extinct in the wild through hunting. Bred in zoos and returned to the wild.
- Mongolian wild horse. Probably extinct in the wild, but bred in zoos.

Animals for which we are too late:

- Passenger pigeon. Hunted to extinction in North America by 1914.
- Quagga. A partly-striped South African zebra. Last one died 1883.
- Blaubok. A South African antelope. Became extinct from hunting in 180(

◄ HABITAT GONE. *This tropical rain forest in the north of Australia has been cut down for a farm. Many animals and plants will be unable to live in the new conditions.*

► HUNTING. *Even in places which are supposed to be set apart for wildlife, some people hunt. Here some poachers have been arrested in Namibia for hunting in a protected area.*

WILDLIFE UNDER THREAT

1 Grey wolf
2 Bald eagle
3 American bison
4 American crocodile
5 Tapir
6 Anaconda
7 Puma
8 Andean condor
9 Maned wolf
10 Harp seal
11 Ermine
12 Lynx
13 Snowy owl
14 Wild boar
15 Golden eagle
16 Nile crocodile
17 Black colobus monkey
18 African elephant
19 Ruffed lemur
20 White rhinoceros
21 Wolverine
22 Brown bear
23 Snow leopard
24 Bengal tiger
25 Dugong
26 Giant panda
27 Green turtle
28 Orang-utang
29 Koala
30 Tasmanian wolf
31 Tuatara
32 Blue whale

◄ POLLUTION *can act slowly or suddenly. This river looks like a pleasant place, but the salmon and trout on the bank have died from pollution. Both kinds of fish need pure water.*

► LOOKING AFTER, *or conservation. At one time the Père David's deer in Woburn, England, were the only ones left. They were bred there and sent to zoos and to China – their proper home.*

EUROPE

Europe is the smallest continent but is joined to the biggest continent, Asia. Most of Europe has a temperate climate – cold temperate in central and eastern Europe, warm temperate in the west and south.

Northwest Europe enjoys a much milder climate than it should for its latitude, or distance away from the Equator. This is because part of the warm ocean current known as the Gulf Stream flows past it.

ANCIENT FORESTS

Thousands of years ago almost the whole of Europe, highlands and lowlands, was heavily forested. A broad belt of conifer trees covered northern Europe. It formed part of the boreal (northern) forest that ringed the northern hemisphere. The rest of Europe, with a milder climate, was covered with forests of broad-leaved deciduous trees, such as oak and chestnut.

▼ **EUROPE** is cut off from Asia in the east by the Ural Mountains. A huge plain covers much of the continent. It extends from the Arctic west to the North Sea and south to Black Sea. There are mountains in the northwest and south. The climate in Europe varies from Arctic in the far north to Mediterranean in the south. Wildlife abounds in most regions, even though Europe is more crowded with people than any other continent.

FOREST REMNANTS

Most of the boreal forest belt still remains. But over the centuries the deciduous forests were gradually wiped out as the population increased and farmers cleared more and more land for crops and livestock. Today only scattered areas of original forest are left. The New Forest near Southampton in southern England is an example.

Most of the native animals in Europe were thus forest-dwellers. Large mammals such as bears, wolves, and wild boars were once found everywhere. Now they are confined to the remote forest regions that remain. The once quite widespread European bison survives only in small herds in zoos and wildlife reserves.

FARMLAND SQUATTERS

Smaller mammals have thrived on the ever expanding farmland of Europe. They include foxes, moles, hedgehogs, hares, and rabbits.

EUROPEAN FEATS

- Blue whale, the world's biggest mammal, can grow to over 100 feet long.
- Pygmy shrew, world's smallest land mammal, weighs 0.1 ounces at most. Its body is 0.2 inches long, and its tail is 0.1 inches.
- Peregrine falcon, fastest bird in the world, can reach speeds of over 155 miles an hour.
- A female field vole can reproduce when only 25 days old and can produce up to 130 young every year.
- Swift, the world's most aerial land bird, remains airborne for up to three years. It eats, drinks, sleeps, and even mates on the wing.
- A male emperor moth can detect the scent of a female over a distance of more than 6 miles.

Mice and rats flourish in town as well as country, living on farm produce and waste food left by animals and people.

GARDENS OF DELIGHT

A host of song birds – blackbirds, thrushes, robins, wrens, sparrows, starlings, and pigeons, also benefit from human influence, nesting and finding a plentiful food supply in our gardens. The warm coasts of Europe provide wintering grounds for huge flocks of geese, waders and other birds that breed in the Arctic.

WILDLIFE AT RISK

Wildlife is still at risk in Europe from farming and industry. Many hedgerows have been destroyed. Other habitats are being ruined by housing and big engineering projects. "Green" measures are being taken in most countries to reduce the threats of pollution and acid rain, but much remains to be done.

▼ *A small tortoiseshell butterfly* settles on a Michaelmas daisy. This is a common European species, seen in great numbers in summer. The insects hibernate in the fall, often going into houses and dry barns.

◄ *A lynx* in a Swiss mountain forest. This beautiful but not often seen "small cat" is a creature of the forests. It is found in Alpine forests and in the great boreal forest that stretches across the north of the continent.

◄ *A group of flamingos* feeding in the Camargue wetlands, in southern France. Strangely, they feed with their bill upside down, filtering tiny creatures from the mud they have stirred up with their feet.

Northern Europe

Northern Europe is about as far away from the Equator as Canada. But it enjoys a much milder climate, thanks to the warm Gulf Stream flowing past. That is why there is only a narrow strip of tundra in the far north of Norway and Russia. It is covered with snow for much of the year. Only in the brief Arctic summer does the snow melt and low vegetation grow.

LONG SUMMER DAYS

The summer growth and long summer daylight attract a host of animals to the tundra. Birds go there in their thousands to nest in the boggy landscape. They include many species of swans, geese, ducks, and waders, such as the whooper swan, white-fronted goose, scaup, and godwit. The birds migrate south to shores, estuaries and other wetlands in the fall.

Herds of reindeer and elk (caribou and moose in North America) roam the tundra in the summer. They are preyed on by wolves and brown bears (grizzly bears in North America). Wild and domesticated reindeer graze the tundra. They also eat rodents, such as voles and lemmings.

▲ *A grass snake* coiled up and basking in the spring sunshine. Grass snakes are one of the commonest reptiles in Europe. They grow to about 47 inches long and are not poisonous.

▼ *A mixed colony of seabirds* on a rocky island in the North Sea. Most of the birds are guillemots, which lay their single egg on the bare rock. The few other birds in the picture, kittiwakes, build nests.

LEMMINGS ON THE RUN

Every few years the lemming populatio becomes enormous, and a mass migratio takes place to find new feeding ground Often the migration turns into a mad par and hordes of animals sometimes ru headlong into rivers or the sea and drown

WINTER SHELTER

In the winter reindeer, bears, and wolv leave the tundra and return to the shelter the thick evergreen boreal forest. The fore is home to many smaller animals, includi foxes, badgers, martens, weasels, and r squirrels. These animals are also found other wooded areas of northern Europ Some are hunted and trapped for their fu to make clothing.

Foxes live in many suburbs, foraging the gardens at night. Red squirrels are bei driven into increasingly remote are because of competition with the bolder gr squirrel, which was introduced into Europ from North America during the last centur Many other species have been introduce including the muntjac deer. It has joined t native roe, fallow and red deer.

▲ *The European hedgehog* is a familiar visitor to gardens, even in towns. It feeds mainly at night on invertebrates, such as earthworms, slugs, and beetles. The stiff spines on the hedgehog's back give it good protection from predators such as foxes. When it is threatened, it rolls up into a ball, with only the spines showing.

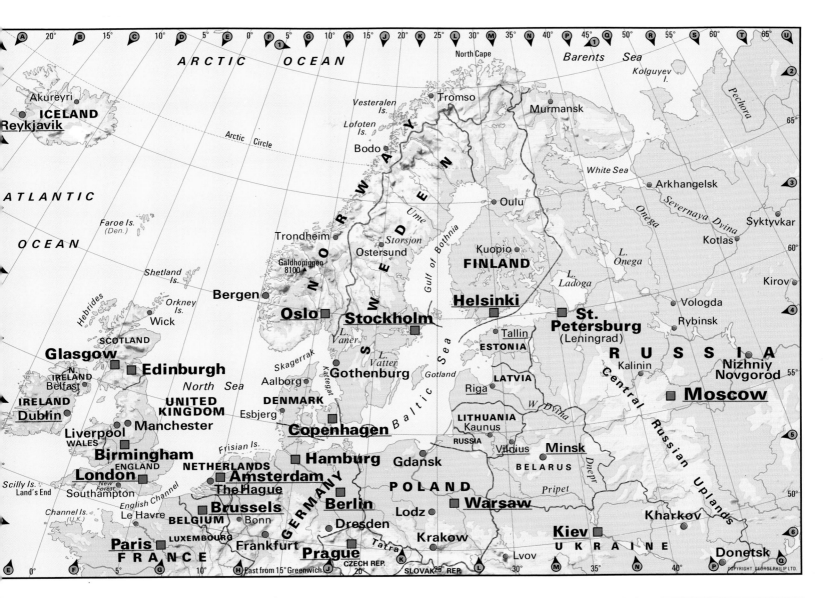

THE LIVING HEDGEROWS

The farmland and hedgerows of the region harbor a staggering variety of wildlife — hedgehogs, moles, mice, shrews, stoats, rats, snakes, rabbits, and hares. Water voles, frogs, toads, and newts are common in freshwater, along with otters and beavers.

Rabbits have again multiplied and reached pest populations in places, after being nearly wiped out by the disease myxomatosis in the 1950s. Hares are renowned for their courting antics in the spring, when they dance and spar with one another.

The forests, farmland, wetlands, and shores of Europe abound with birds. Tits, finches, thrushes, blackbirds, robins, swifts, swallows, and house martins are among the commonest birds. The last three are migrants. In the spring they fly in from their winter feeding grounds in Africa to breed and return there in the fall. The biggest wetland birds are herons and storks, which feed on fish and amphibians.

▲ **IN THE NORTH** of the region lies a narrow expanse of tundra. South of the tundra is the boreal forest, which gives way to a huge area of fertile plains.

▼ **Wolves** are social animals, that is, they live in packs. There is a definite "pecking order" in wolf society. A lower member of the pack greets a higher member with ears lowered and tail down.

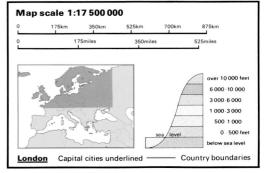

Map scale 1:17 500 000

0	175km	350km	525km	700km	875km

0	175miles	350miles	525miles

over 10 000 feet
6 000-10 000
3 000-6 000
1 000-3 000
500-1 000
0-500 feet
sea level
below sea level

London Capital cities underlined ——— Country boundaries

Southern Europe

Southern Europe includes many of the lands bordering the Mediterranean Sea. It has a very pleasant climate that attracts millions of vacationers every year. The summers are hot and dry with clear skies, and the winters are warm and wet. This type of climate, called a Mediterranean climate, is not common. It is found elsewhere only on the Californian coast of North America and in parts of southern Australia.

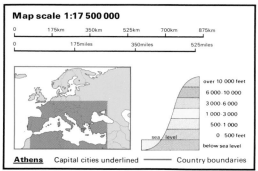

Map scale 1:17 500 000

| 0 | 175km | 350km | 525km | 700km | 875km |

| 0 | 175miles | 350miles | 525miles |

over 10 000 feet
6 000 - 10 000
3 000 - 6 000
1 000 - 3 000
500 - 1 000
0 - 500 feet
below sea level
sea level

Athens Capital cities underlined ——— Country boundaries

UNNATURAL LANDSCAPE

The climate becomes dramatically cooler, however, in the mountains of the Pyrenees and the Alps. The Alps have peaks that are snow-covered all year.

Because human beings have lived in the region for so long, they have totally altered the natural landscape. They have cut down the original forest trees to create farmland and have planted trees such as olives instead.

Some of the original kinds of trees can be found in places. They include the maritime and aleppo pines and the cork oak. Corks are made from the bark of the cork oak, an evergreen that can live up to 400 years.

▼ **SOUTHERN EUROPE** borders the Mediterranean Sea. The surrounding lands enjoy a warm temperate climate, with hot, dry summers and mild, wet winters. There are mountains in most countries.

BEARS, BIRDS, BEETLES

The brown bear appears on all the Yugoslav stamps. It is becoming rare everywhere and is in danger.

This explains why these stamps include the panda symbol of the WWF (World Wildlife Fund). The French stamps show two of the many beetles of the warm south. The bird on the Gibraltar stamp is the scavenging black kite.

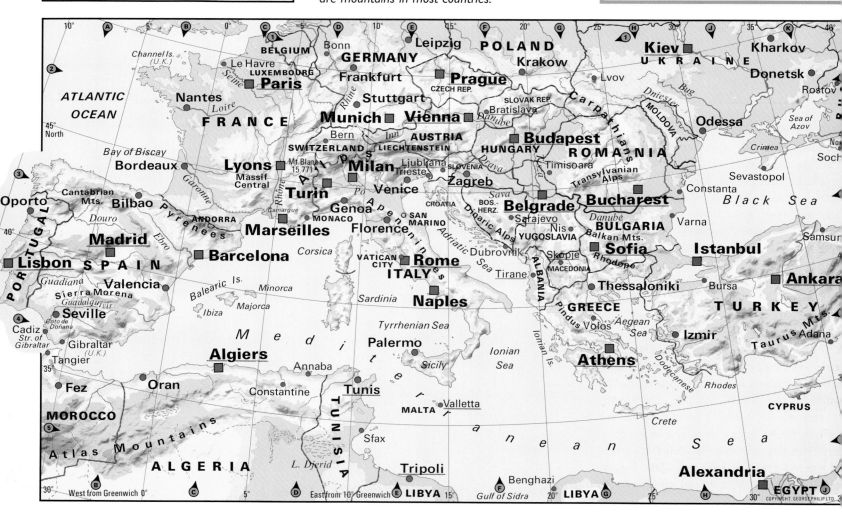

MAQUIS AND GARRIGUE

Most of the Mediterranean region has now been reduced to arid scrubland. The typical vegetation in most parts is tough-leaved evergreen shrubs, bushes and small trees. There are aromatic (sweet-smelling) shrubs such as oregano and thyme, with laurels, myrtles, brooms, olives, and figs. When the vegetation is dense, it is known as the *maquis*; when more open, the *garrigue*.

Many lizards, snakes, and tortoises live in the scrub, but it has few large wild animals because of overgrazing by sheep and goats. Some wild sheep like the mouflon are to be found in the highlands on Corsica and Sardinia and in the Alps.

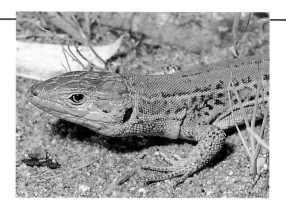

▲ *A Balkan wall lizard is one of many lizards found in the Mediterranean region. Like most cold-blooded animals, it comes to life in the daytime heat. As its name suggests, it is a skillful climber, like the gecko.*

◄ *Mouflon wild sheep climbing a mountain slope in the Austrian Alps. They are the smallest wild sheep, with large curved horns. They thrive not only in Europe, but also in cold deserts in Asia.*

► *One kind of rhinoceros beetle, spotted on a dead tree in southern France. There is no need to wonder how it got its name! The males use the curved "horn" for fighting to win a female to mate with.*

MOUNTAIN GOATS

Nimble ibex and chamois (rock goats), which are renowned for their leaping ability, are also highland creatures of the Pyrenees and Alps. Wolves and eagles are among their main predators.

SOUTHERN WETLANDS

While most of the coasts of the region are bordered by scrubland, some are marshy. Two notable large wetland areas are the Camargue in southern France and the Coto Doñana in southern Spain. Both are under threat by reclamation projects to produce more farmland.

The Camargue is famed for its wild horses and extensive birdlife, particularly flamingos and egrets. It is also one of the last remaining refuges for European beavers and rare water turtles.

Half the bird species in Europe are found in the Coto Doñana. They include flamingos, egrets, terns, shelducks, marsh harriers, and the rare Spanish imperial eagle. The Spanish lynx is one of the rare mammals.

▲ **EAGLE-EYED.** The eagle owl has just caught a wood pigeon. This owl is a large bird, up to 28 inches long. It has ear tufts and large orange eyes, which help it to see well in the dark. It has a particularly loud hoot, which can be heard 3 miles away and is a signal to its neighbors.

Eastern Europe

This region of Europe is occupied by parts of Russia, the Baltic States, Belarus, Ukraine, Poland, the Slovak Republic, Hungary, Romania, Moldova, and Bulgaria. The landscape is mainly flat except for the Central Russian Uplands.

The River Volga, which drains half of the Russian lowlands, flows into the Caspian Sea. It is Europe's longest river, 2,295 miles long. Poland is mainly flat, too, but the other countries are quite mountainous.

FOREST AND STEPPE

Three major vegetation regions cover eastern Europe's lowlands. The generally evergreen forest in the north is the southern part of the great boreal forest (see page 24). Further south the forest and grassland mix together to create the forest-steppe, which transforms gradually into open steppe. The steppe grasslands are equivalent to the prairies in North America. They provide rich grazing for livestock and fertile land for growing cereals, like wheat and oats, and other crops.

BISON, HAMSTERS, BUSTARDS

The forest-steppe was once the home of great herds of wisent, or European bison. This looks much like the American bison, or buffalo. It became extinct in the wild early this century. Small herds still exist, however, in nature reserves in Poland and elsewhere in eastern Europe.

The most plentiful wildlife on the open steppe are rodents. They include ground squirrels like marmots and susliks, mouse-like jerboas, and hamsters. The golden hamster is the species that millions of children keep as pets. Like the common hamster, it stores food in its cheek pouches. Wild hamsters, however, can be very fierce.

The great bustard is one of the largest birds on the steppe. It spends most of its time on the ground but can fly powerfully. The male has a notable courtship display, inflating its neck like a balloon and fanning out its wing and tail feathers. Grouse, quail, and larks are also common. Eagles, hawks, falcons, and kites are the main birds of prey.

THE ALPINE SYSTEM

The Carpathian Mountains run in an arc through the Slovak Republic and Romania. They belong to the same mountain system as the Alps but are much lower. The higher Caucasus Mountains in southeast Russia are also part of the system. They have Mt. Elbrus (18,481 feet), the highest peak in Europe.

Much of the mountainous land is heavily forested. There is deciduous woodland of oak, beech, and ash on the lower slopes and evergreen firs, spruce, and pine higher up. In the Caucasus Mountains the climate of the foothills is subtropical. Bamboo, laurel, and palm trees flourish there.

BIG BEAVER

The European beaver is the largest rodent in Europe. It can measure more than 5 feet from nose to tail. It waddles clumsily on land, but moves gracefully in the water, propelling itself with its webbed hind feet. European beavers look like North American beavers but are much rarer.

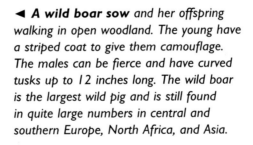

◄ *A wild boar sow* and her offspring walking in open woodland. The young have a striped coat to give them camouflage. The males can be fierce and have curved tusks up to 12 inches long. The wild boar is the largest wild pig and is still found in quite large numbers in central and southern Europe, North Africa, and Asia.

▼ *THE DAM BUILDERS.* Beavers build their lodge (home) in the middle of a pond or at the water's edge. This is so that they can have an entrance underwater, making the lodge safe from land predators. They often create a deep pond by damming a stream with sticks, stones, and mud. They build up the dam until the water level behind it is high enough. The beaver's lodge is cone-shaped and also made of sticks, stones, and mud.

Lodge or house

Entrance

Dam

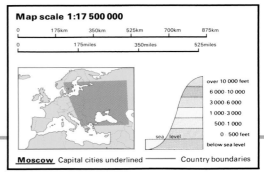

Map scale 1:17 500 000

| 0 | 175km | 350km | 525km | 700km | 875km |
| 0 | 175miles | 350miles | 525miles |

over 10 000 feet
6 000-10 000
3 000-6 000
1 000-3 000
500-1 000
0-500 feet
below sea level

Moscow Capital cities underlined — Country boundaries

HIGHLAND LIFE

In the mountain forests live brown bears, wolves, lynxes, squirrels, wild boar, and wild goats. Among goat-like species are the chamois and, in the Caucasus, the tur, which is closely related to the wider-ranging ibex.

The high mountains are also the home of the alpine marmot. This thickset, thick-coated and bushy-tailed rodent is the largest member of the squirrel family. It lives in large colonies on the ground. In winter it hibernates in its burrow with other members of its family. Bears, foxes, and eagles prey on marmots.

◄ **EASTERN EUROPE** is mostly lowland. But there are mountain chains in the south – the Carpathians and the Caucasus. Most of the region has cold winters and hot summers. The Black Sea coast has a milder climate and is a popular resort area.

Red deer make their home in deciduous woodlands and open moorland. One of the largest deer, they are found in other parts of Europe and also in North Africa and Asia. Only the males have antlers.

A red squirrel eats with its forepaws. It feeds on conifer seeds, nuts, and berries and also on insects and birds' eggs. Red squirrels are found in conifer and mixed forests throughout the region and elsewhere in Europe. They nest in the trees.

ASIA

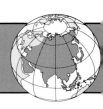

Asia is the biggest of the continents. It occupies just less than a third of the Earth's total land area. The Ural Mountains in the west mark the boundary between Asia and Europe. Sometimes Europe and Asia are considered as one supercontinent, Eurasia.

Much of the continent is wilderness and is sparsely populated. The far north reaches into the Arctic and is snow-covered for much of the year. Moving south, there is a broad band of conifer forest. The forest gives way to grassy plains called the steppe.

MOUNTAINS AND DESERT

Further south, as the climate warms, the steppe merges into arid deserts. From them rise great mountain chains, including the Himalayas. In the far west, beyond the Gulf, is the scorching desert of the Arabian peninsula.

East of the Himalayas and the high, cold Tibetan Plateau lies China, which is mostly steppe and desert. South of the Himalayas is the subcontinent of India, most of which lies in the tropics. Two great rivers, the Indus and the Ganges, water the continent and bring life to the land. The climate gets hotter and wetter going south into the equatorial islands of Indonesia and Borneo.

▲ **The moon moth**, one of the most beautiful of all moths, settles on a fern in a Malaysian rain forest. Moon, or luna, moths are noted for the shape of their wings and their long "tail."

▼ **An Indian rhinoceros** grazes in its favorite swampland habitat. It is the heaviest of the three species of Asian rhino, all of which have one horn.

RANGING NEAR AND FAR

Because the continent is so large, t wildlife varies enormously from region region, as the map shows. Some species ha a wide range. For example, the rhes monkey roams from Afghanistan, throu India, to China. Other species have a ve limited range because of the particu habitat they prefer. Some are found only a single island, such as the proboscis monk on Borneo.

WEALTH OF WILDLIFE

In forested tropical regions, there are:
- Tigers, biggest of the "big cats"
- Apes (gibbons), whose males and females sing tuneful duets
- Pythons up to 32 feet long
- Tapirs, which look like a cross betwee a rhinoceros, a horse, and a pig
- Birdwing butterflies, with wings more than 10 inches across
- Rafflesia plants, with flowers more tha 3 feet across
- Spice trees, which yield cloves, nutme mace, and cinnamon.

The habitats of many tropical species a now at risk from logging and agriculture.

CROCODILE MUGGERS

Crocodiles thrive throughout tropical Asia. They are fearsome predators that attack animals as large as buffalos. The saltwater, or estuarine, crocodile is widespread and grows up to 20 feet long. The marsh crocodile (below) lives in swamps in southern India.

ASIA is a sprawling landmass that tends from the Arctic Ocean to beyond e Equator. Much of the land consists of ld plains and plateaus, steppes, or hot, dry serts. The high Tibetan Plateau and even gher Himalayas form a formidable barrier wildlife. Most plants and animals live in the pical south and southeast of the region.

The infinite variety of Asia's wildlife is reflected in its stamps. The chirping of crickets can be deafening in the tropics, while in tropical waters garishly colored fish swim around the reefs. Big and small cats like the snow leopard and the caracal prefer cooler climates.

33

North Asia

The Russian region of Siberia occupies all of northern Asia. It covers almost a third of the continent, but hardly anyone lives there. This is not surprising because most of the region is cold and desolate. The north lies well within the Arctic Circle. It has the typical treeless tundra landscape of the Arctic lands in Europe and North America. And it has much the same kinds of wildlife.

LIFE ON THE TUNDRA

Polar bears hunt seals on the ice floes in the Arctic Ocean, in which fish, narwhals, and killer whales swim. There is little life on the tundra in the long, bitterly cold winter. Arctic foxes and hares venture there from the forest further south. Ptarmigan, willow grouse, and snowy owls are among the birds that winter on the tundra.

▼ BUSY BURROWERS

Several species of burrowing rodents are found on the plains and steppes of the region. Each excavates a different kind of burrow. Lemmings dig quite shallow burrows. Hamsters dig deeper and may hibernate in their burrows. So do marmots and susliks. Mole rats are the best burrowers.

The snowy owl preys on another winter resident, the arctic lemming, the only lemming to grow a white camouflage coat in winter. It burrows beneath the snow to escape the severest cold. Other lemmings and their relatives the voles live in the conifer forests and steppe further south.

In summer, when the snow melts and the grass starts to grow, the tundra really comes to life. Migrant birds flock there to breed from their wintering grounds in southern and western Europe and Asia. They include the dark brent goose and the gray bean goose, plus Bewick's swans and waders like sandpipers, plovers, and stints.

CARNIVORE GLUTTON

The tundra gives way in the south to the biggest region of forest in the world. It is part of the boreal (northern) forest belt that girdles the northern hemisphere. Larch, pine, and spruce are the main conifer tree species. Hardy deciduous trees, such as aspen and birch, grow in some areas.

Compared with the tundra, the fore region, called taiga, teems with life. It is t home of carnivores such as the brown bea lynx, wolf, wolverine and, within wate habitats, the river otter. The brown bear becoming increasingly rare. The wolverin also called glutton, is a small bear-like anim with a very bushy coat and tail. Despite appearance and its name, it is not related the bear or the wolf. Weasels and poleca are its closest relatives.

BLIND DIGGERS

Mole rats live in the southwest of the region and also around the Black Sea and eastern Mediterranean. They are brilliant burrowers, well adapted for a life underground. Their eyes are covered with skin, so they are blind. Their front teeth protrude from their mouth even when it is closed. Each animal digs a separate tunnel system. It excavates separate chambers for a nest and for storing bulbs and vegetables to eat. From there, tunnels lead off to its feeding grounds. The system may be over 1,000 feet long.

Marmot

Suslik

Lemming

Mole rat

Hamster

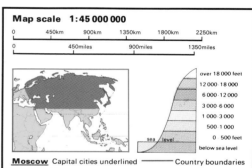

Map scale   1:45 000 000

| 0 | 450km | 900km | 1350km | 1800km | 2250km |

| 0 | 450miles | 900miles | 1350miles |

over 18 000 feet
12 000-18 000
6 000-12 000
3 000-6 000
1 000-3 000
500-1 000
sea level   0-500 feet
below sea level

Moscow Capital cities underlined ——— Country boundaries

A Himalayan black bear stretches up
get at the upper branches of a sapling. It
refers a forest habitat and is a good climber.
makes a platform in the trees to rest, using
ranches it has broken while feeding.

▲ *NORTHERN ASIA* stretches east from
the Ural Mountains to the North Pacific
Ocean. It is bounded in the south by high
mountain chains. The whole region belongs
to Russia. Most of it is a cold wilderness.

HUNTED FOR FUR
The wolverine is hunted for its fur. So
are other members of the weasel family that
live in the Russian taiga. They include the
stoat, or ermine, and the sable (a kind of
marten).

ON THE STEPPE
South of the taiga, the grass-covered steppe
begins. This is the equivalent of the prairie in
North America. It becomes more arid
toward the south. Being in the middle of the
continent, the steppe is very cold in winter
but very hot in summer.

Burrowing rodents are common on the
steppe. Among them are marmots and
susliks. These are ground squirrels, similar to
the prairie dogs of North America. The chief
grazers of the steppe are antelopes, like the
saiga antelope, with its big snout.

Middle East

The Middle East is the name usually given to Southwest Asia. Most of the region is very dry and includes one of the greatest desert regions in the world, occupying almost all of the Arabian Peninsula between the Red Sea and the Persian Gulf.

Individual deserts in the region include the Rub 'al Khali ("the empty quarter") in the south. In its huge, barren sandy wastes, temperatures can rise to 122°F or more.

DESERT OASES

The vast deserts seem almost lifeless. What life there is appears to be concentrated in the oases dotted here and there. These are places where underground water bubbles to the surface. The typical tree of the oasis is the date palm, whose fruit feeds humans and wild animals alike. Oasis pools contain small fish and provide homes for amphibians, such as frogs and salamanders.

Rain does fall in many parts of the desert, mainly in winter. When this happens, buried seeds germinate, flower, and seed in days, making the desert bloom for a short while.

ADAPTABLE GERBILS

That popular pet, the gerbil, is a creature of the desert. Its wild relatives live throughout the Middle East, as well as in Africa and central Asia. They are well adapted to the arid environment. They forage for seeds at night when the seeds are soaked with dew. So when they eat, they drink as well.

▶ *HOT SANDY DESERT and semidesert cover most of the Middle East. Along the Mediterranean coast there is scattered woodland and scrub. Thick forests grow in the wetter mountainous areas to the north.*

▲ *This cryptic beetle is well camouflaged for life in the Negev Desert. It is one of the darkling beetles, so called because they generally search for food at night.*

JUMPING JERBOAS

Jerboas are another family of desert roden with short front feet and long back feet th they use for jumping. They burrow as dee as 6.5 feet to escape the daytime heat. A well as most seeds and vegetation, jerbo eat insects.

INSECTS AND SNAKES

A variety of flies, fleas, and beetles live in th desert. They include the dung beetle, whic eats and lays its eggs in balls of animal dun Predatory insects called mantids prey o other insects. They camouflage themselve as twigs or even pebbles. The most dead creatures of the desert are scorpions ar snakes. Some of them can kill humans.

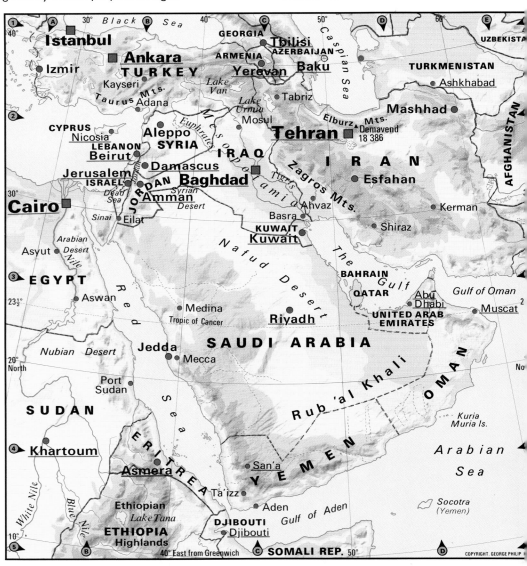

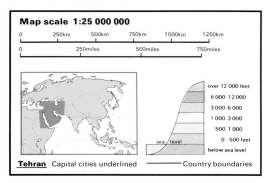

Map scale 1:25 000 000

0	250km	500km	750km	1000km	1250km

0	250miles	500miles	750miles

over 12 000 feet
6 000 12 000
3 000 6 000
1 000 3 000
500 1 000
0 500 feet
sea level
below sea level

<u>Tehran</u> Capital cities underlined ▬▬▬ Country boundaries

BIG EARS

Because of the extreme heat, relatively few large mammals live in the desert. The classic desert dweller is the camel, which is so well adapted for desert life. Several members of the dog family also inhabit different parts of the region, including hyenas, jackals, and foxes. Well known is the desert, or fennec, fox, the smallest of all the foxes. It has enormous ears, which help radiate away body heat. They also give it acute hearing to detect insect prey.

The desert would appear to be the last place for grazing animals, such as the antelope. But one species, the Arabian oryx, can eke out an existence there. It once used to roam throughout the Middle East but became extinct in the wild in the 1970s due to overhunting. However, a group of animals raised in captivity was released into central Oman in 1982 and appears to be flourishing.

Wild cyclamen bloom in springtime in hilly region of Israel. A spur-thighed tortoise saunters by, enjoying the warm sunlight. This tortoise is a popular pet in Europe and may live for 100 years or more.

DESERT DASSIE

This animal, pictured near the salty Dead Sea, is a bit of a puzzle. It's sometimes called a rock rabbit, but it's not a rabbit. In fact it's a dassie, or rock hyrax. Even "hyrax" is not a good name for it because this means "shrew-mouse" in Greek. And the animal isn't like a shrew or a mouse! The dassie isn't like any other animal. Some zoologists believe its closest relative is the elephant!

▼ SHIPS OF THE DESERT.

Arabian camels walk in line through the desert. They are adapted for desert life. They can go for days without drinking water, but they then gulp over 26 gallons at one time! Camels eat all kinds of plants, even the toughest thorny ones. They store food as fat inside their hump. Camels are notoriously bad tempered. They spit, bite, and kick one another and people when annoyed.

South Asia

India occupies most of southern Asia. To the west, Afghanistan and much of Pakistan is rugged, mountainous country. Fertile plains lie south of the Himalayas.

The northern plains are a rich farming area. So is the Deccan, a huge plateau that covers most of tropical India. The Deccan has many areas of thick forest of tropical hardwoods such as teak and rosewood. It is greatly watered in the rainy season. An annual rainfall of 5 feet is not uncommon.

JUNGLE ANIMALS

The forests are alive with all manner of wildlife – macaque monkeys like the rhesus, wild pigs, mongooses, small cats and big cats, elephants, and thousands of species of birds and insects. The Indian, or Asian, elephant is somewhat smaller than its African relative, but still can reach up to 5 tons in weight. The Indian rhinoceros, now rare and restricted to nature reserves, is another heavy-weight. Tigers are quite rare, too. They prey mainly on cattle, deer, and wild pigs. When old or wounded, they may become man-eaters.

▼ *A pair of painted storks* on their rough nest of sticks in southern India. They have mainly white plumage, with black on the breast and wings, which are also tipped with pink. Note the bald head.

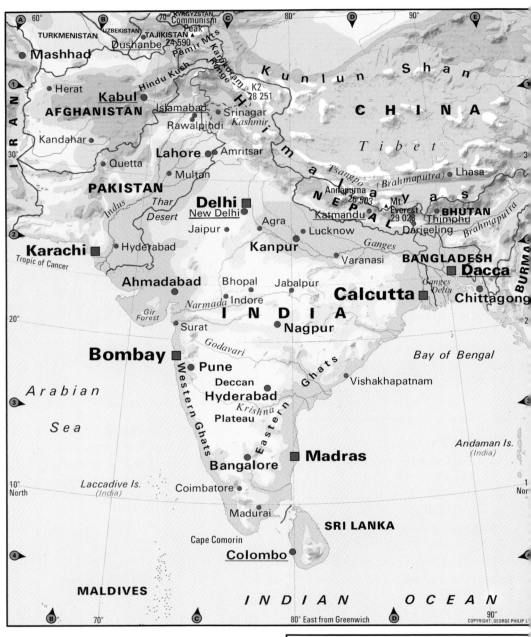

▲ **HIGH MOUNTAIN RANGES** (the Hindu Kush and the Himalayas) form the northern boundary of the region. Going south, the mountains give way to well-watered plains and drier plateaus. Most of the country has heavy monsoon rains from June to September, but it is largely dry at other times.

▶ **The golden palm civet** is found only in Sri Lanka, but the fishing cat ranges into equatorial regions. Civets mostly live in and among trees. The fishing cat feeds on fish, shellfish, birds, and insects.

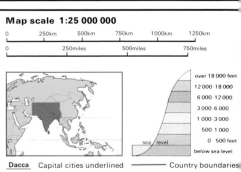

Map scale 1:25 000 000

over 18 000 feet
12 000·18 000
6 000·12 000
3 000·6 000
1 000·3 000
500·1 000
0 500 feet
sea level
below sea level

Dacca Capital cities underlined ——— Country boundaries

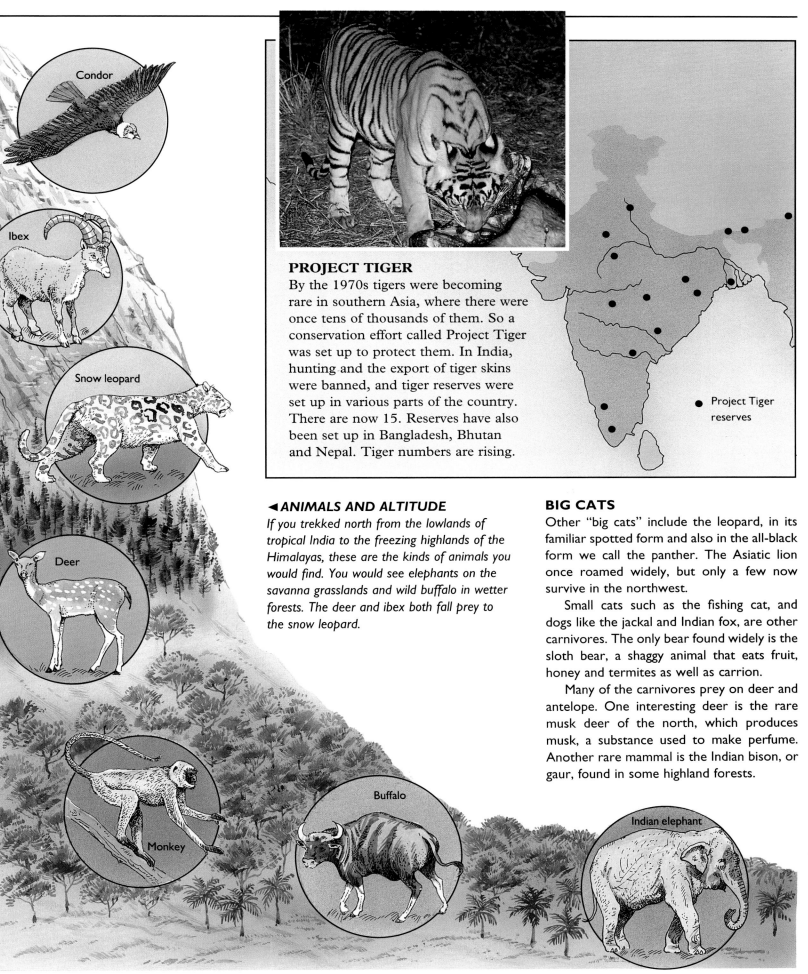

PROJECT TIGER

By the 1970s tigers were becoming rare in southern Asia, where there were once tens of thousands of them. So a conservation effort called Project Tiger was set up to protect them. In India, hunting and the export of tiger skins were banned, and tiger reserves were set up in various parts of the country. There are now 15. Reserves have also been set up in Bangladesh, Bhutan and Nepal. Tiger numbers are rising.

● Project Tiger reserves

Condor

Ibex

Snow leopard

Deer

Monkey

Buffalo

Indian elephant

◄ANIMALS AND ALTITUDE

If you trekked north from the lowlands of tropical India to the freezing highlands of the Himalayas, these are the kinds of animals you would find. You would see elephants on the savanna grasslands and wild buffalo in wetter forests. The deer and ibex both fall prey to the snow leopard.

BIG CATS

Other "big cats" include the leopard, in its familiar spotted form and also in the all-black form we call the panther. The Asiatic lion once roamed widely, but only a few now survive in the northwest.

Small cats such as the fishing cat, and dogs like the jackal and Indian fox, are other carnivores. The only bear found widely is the sloth bear, a shaggy animal that eats fruit, honey and termites as well as carrion.

Many of the carnivores prey on deer and antelope. One interesting deer is the rare musk deer of the north, which produces musk, a substance used to make perfume. Another rare mammal is the Indian bison, or gaur, found in some highland forests.

East Asia

East Asia is a region of hot deserts, cold deserts and well-watered flood plains. The sandy Takla Makan Desert and the more rocky Gobi Desert lie in the north. The Gobi experiences extreme temperatures: 104°F in summer and −40°F in winter. In the driest areas there are only scattered plants, but in the better watered semidesert, or steppe, grass and small bushes grow.

GOBI WILDLIFE

The Bactrian camel, unlike its Arabian cousin, has two humps. It grows a thick, shaggy coat in winter. Only about a thousand now remain in the wild. Even rarer is Przewalski's horse, believed to be one of the original wild horses. It has now been reintroduced into parts of the region after nearly becoming extinct in the 1960s. Other grazing animals include the Mongolian gazelle and the saiga antelope. Rodents such as marmots, sand rats, jirds, and gerbils are common desert dwellers.

TOP OF THE WORLD

The whole southwest of the region is occupied by the high Tibetan Plateau, which is ringed in the south by the Himalayas. Thick forests in Tibet's valleys contain an enormous variety of trees and shrubs — willow, poplar, juniper, pine, oak, bamboo, rhododendrons, and azaleas.

Perhaps surprisingly, Tibet and the Himalayas have a rich wildlife. Shaggy yaks forage at a great height. The increasingly rare snow leopard is a fierce predator of wild sheep and goats. Monkeys are even found in the Himalayas: hanuman, or gray, langurs in the south, and macaques. The rhesus macaque ranges into China, along with other macaques.

▼ *A group of Asian elephants* treks along the riverside. The Asian elephant is smaller than the African. Easily trained, it is used widely in the region and in timber forests in Burma and Thailand in southeast Asia.

▲ *A reticulated python* glides along a branch. Found in the tropics from Burma south to Malaysia, it can grow as long as 32 feet, and is the world's longest snake. It is a constrictor, which means it crushes its prey to death. It feeds mainly on small mammals and on birds. In some farming areas it is a welcome visitor as it kills crop pests such as rats and mice. It can locate prey in darkness by their body heat.

Hardy yaks graze on a mountain slope Nepal. These dark-coated wild cattle thrive roughout the Himalayas and on the Tibetan ateau. They can be found as high as 19,700 et, where few other creatures can survive.

FINE FEATHERS

Few birds can rival the gaudy plumage of the pheasant featured on this Chinese stamp (bottom). They have fine tail feathers, as has the long-tailed broadbill of Vietnam (top). China and Indochina are the original home of many species.

RECIOUS PANDAS

hina's most celebrated animal is the giant anda. It lives in the remote mountains in the outhwest, feeding only on bamboo shoots. has to move on when the bamboo dies. his is more difficult these days because rmland has expanded into their territory. a result, the pandas are on the verge of xtinction. A lesser known panda, the red anda, also lives in China and in the imalayas. It, too, is a bamboo-eater and is nder threat.

APANESE CHERRIES

pan is a mountainous country, with many road-leaved and conifer forests. It is noted articularly for its fine flowering cherry ees. The country has its own species of acaque, which is very hardy. It grows a ick coat to survive the cold, snowy winters f northern Japan. The forests are also the ome of the sacred Japanese sika deer.

▲ FARMLAND AND RIVERS

Mountains, steppe and desert cover more than two-thirds of the region. Few people live in this vast area. Much of what remains is fertile farmland, which is intensively cultivated and supports China's vast population. The farmland is centered on two main rivers, the Hwang Ho and the Yangtze. They rise in the Tibetan Plateau and flood regularly. The region has heavy monsoon rain in summer.

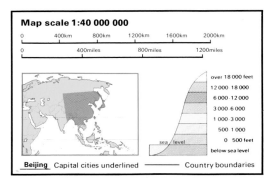

Map scale 1:40 000 000

Beijing Capital cities underlined — Country boundaries

Southeast Asia

Southeast Asia is a heavily forested region. Literally thousands of species of trees grow in the highland and lowland forests. One of the most important timber trees is teak, which is felled and extracted with the help of elephants in several countries. Rattan palms, bamboo, and even oak, laurel, and conifers grow in different areas. Rubber trees are cultivated on a very large scale, particularly in Malaysia. They were brought here from South America in the 1870s. The tree bark is cut to get latex.

OILS AND SPICES

Among the more interesting trees is the camphor tree, which yields a fragrant oil. The sandalwood tree produces a fragrant wood used for carving and to make incense. The Indonesian islands in particular are noted for their spice trees, which include clove, nutmeg, and cinnamon.

STRANGE AND BEAUTIFUL

The trees in the forest are entangled with lianas, the thick climbing vines. Hosts of epiphytes, or air plants, grow in the moist and mossy tree crevices. The most beautiful of them are orchids of all shapes, sizes, and colors. But for sheer spectacle nothing can beat the rafflesia. This is a parasitic plant that grows on vines in Malaysia and Indonesia. It has no stem or leaves, just a huge flower. The biggest blooms can grow to 3 feet across.

ORANGUTANS UNDER THREAT

The forest and jungles of Southeast Asia are rich in animal life, from twig-like stick insects to orangutans, distant relatives of ourselves. This large ape lives only in Sumatra and Borneo and, like many other species in the region, is threatened by the wholesale destruction of its habitat.

MEAT-EATING PLANTS

The pitcher plants of Southeast Asia are one kind of carnivorous plant: they feed on animal life. The sundew and Venus's-flytrap are two others. Pitcher plants attract insects to their water-filled pitchers with sweet-smelling nectar. The insects lose their footing on the slippery lip of the pitchers, fall in, and drown. The plant then digests them to obtain the nutrients they need.

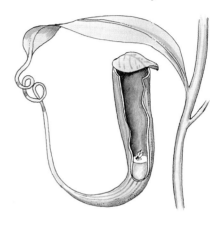

▲ *A millipede scurries across a tree trunk in a Malaysian forest, with its legs moving in a kind of rippling wave. The word millipede means "thousand feet." Count how many pairs of feet this one has. Millipedes spend most time on the forest floor, feeding on decaying leaf litter.*

▶ *Water-filled "pitchers" on a pitcher plant in Borneo. At least 20 species of the plant grow in the damp tropical forests on the island. Others are found on neighboring islands and in the Philippines. The "pitchers" on the plant are special leaves that curl round to make a watertight vessel. They act as pitfalls to trap insects such as ants and flies.*

BORNEO SPECIALS

Borneo is also the only habitat for the proboscis monkey, known for the fleshy tongue-like nose of the male. But other monkeys, including various macaques, leaf monkeys, and surelis, are more common.

Two great "leapers" also inhabit the island forests. The tarsier is a primitive primate. The flying lemur is a squirrel-like mammal with skin between its limbs. It can glide from tree to tree.

"HERE BE DRAGONS!"

Among the bigger animals, Asian elephants are found throughout the region. Tigers are rare, and rhinoceros even rarer. About 150 of the two-horned Sumatran rhino are left on the mainland and on Sumatra itself. The island of Komodo is the home of the quite unique Komodo dragon. This giant lizard can be nearly 13 feet long. It preys on large mammals, including deer and wild pigs and is believed to have killed people. It is fast moving, can climb trees, and is a good swimmer.

The spectacular bloom of a ground orchid in a tropical forest on Mt. Kinabalu on the island of Borneo. Most tropical orchid species are found in forested mountain regions rather than in low-level rain forests.

Female long-tailed macaques enjoy a grooming session, and so strengthen family bonds. These macaques live in Java. Others are found on other islands in Indonesia. They prefer the forest edge near rivers and coasts.

▲ *Spot the cricket!* Bush-crickets like this are found widely in the tropical forests of the region. They protect themselves from enemies like frogs and birds by mimicking, or looking like, leaves or twigs. How well they do it!

▼ *SOUTHEAST ASIA* lies in the tropics. The mainland experiences seasonal wet and dry monsoons. But the islands of Indonesia and Borneo, which straddle the Equator, have heavy rainfall all year round.

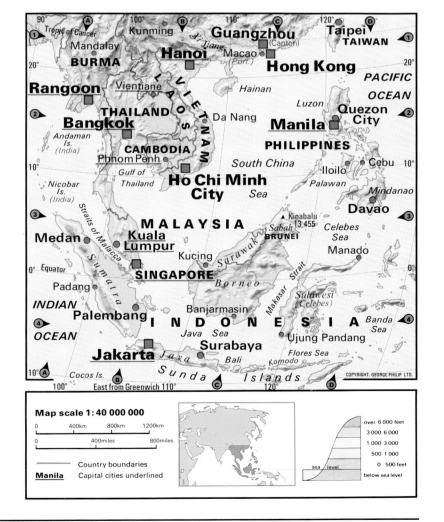

Map scale 1: 40 000 000

| 0 | 400km | 800km | 1200km |

| 0 | 400miles | 800miles |

———— Country boundaries

Manila Capital cities underlined

over 6 000 feet
3 000-6 000
1 000-3 000
500-1 000
0-500 feet
below sea level

AFRICA

Africa is the continent where the first humans lived, but many parts are still surprisingly empty of people. Large areas are desert, but other regions can be difficult for people to live in too. Even today, though, there are areas of Africa where wildlife is plentiful. On some African savannas you can see huge herds of zebras and antelopes such as wildebeest. There are lions, cheetahs, giraffes, and, where they have not been killed for tusks and horns, elephants and rhinoceroses. African savannas must be one of the best parts of the world for wildlife watching.

FOREST GLIMPSES

Forest creatures are much harder to see. Plenty of animals live there, but many are good at hiding. They need to be to survive – either to avoid being eaten or to stalk their prey without being seen.

Down on the forest floor, you may be able to move around freely because many parts have little undergrowth. But it can be very gloomy, and your chance of seeing animals, before they see or hear you and move away, is not great. Many animals live out of sight in the treetops. You may only catch glimpses of them. Birds flit from branch to branch. Branches shake as animals such as squirrels move along them fast.

▲ **A male red-billed weaver** emerges from his nest. Most weaver birds live in Africa. They build nests out of strands of grass, which are woven into a ball, often with an entrance for protection. Many weavers live in colonies, so a whole tree may be covered with their nests on almost every twig.

▼ **The greater kudu** is just one of over 70 species of antelope that live in Africa. It lives in scrub and woods, often in hilly places, but cannot go without water for too long. These are all females. Males have long spiral horns.

▲ **A painted reed frog** calls to attract a mate. This frog belongs to a family with 290 species. All of them live in Africa south of the Sahara or in Madagascar. Many are good climbers and brightly colored.

Crashing branches in the distance signal th. some monkeys have been disturbed ar have left their feeding area in a hurry.

TEEMING FORESTS

A belt of forest runs across the center Africa and along part of the east coast. contains a huge number of animals. But fe of them live in large groups. Forest antelope like the bongo move quietly through th

AFRICAN RECORD BREAKERS
- The biggest desert (Sahara – 2,100,000 square miles)
- The longest river (Nile – 4,150 miles)
- The tallest animal (giraffe – up to 20 feet)
- The heaviest land animal (African elephant – up to 6 tons)
- The biggest bird (ostrich – nearly 10 feet tall)
- The biggest ape (gorilla – up to 400 pounds in weight)
- The fastest land animal (cheetah – 60 miles an hour)
- The biggest insect (Goliath beetle – 8 inches long, 3.5 ounces)

rest alone. Leopards hunt singly. Forest
rds include hornbills, eagles, sunbirds,
rrots, and many others. There are frogs,
ards, snakes, and insects.

ESERT DWELLERS
the desert a relatively small number of
nimals are spread out over a wide area. But
frica, the only continent with antelopes, has
veral kinds adapted to live here, like the

addax and Dorcas gazelle. The eastern tip
of Africa has much semidesert and scrub.
Somali wild asses and the dibatag, a gazelle
that stands on its hind legs to feed, are able
to survive here.

In the Sahara are oases and mountain
areas. They may have baboons, toads, and
other animals not found in drier places. The
northern part of Africa above the Sahara has
Mediterranean-type animals.

▲ WILDLIFE OF AFRICA
*Large areas of tropical forest, savanna, and
desert cover much of the continent. They
are not quite so solid as the map shows.
Where rivers run through the savanna they
may have forested banks. There are clearings
in the forest and oases in the desert. Many
African animals live nowhere else in the wild.
Examples include the giraffe, okapi, aardvark,
hippopotamus, and springhare.*

North Africa

This region is one of the driest in the world, but there are places where water may be found. In the east, there is a huge river, the Nile, and another in the south, the Niger. A vast swamp, the Sudd, lies in southern Sudan, and there are oases dotted across the desert. Some of the northern coast also has rain for part of the year.

A CHANGED LAND

The Sahara Desert takes up most of the region. But this part of Africa was not always a barren place. The swings in climate that came with the Ice Ages gave it for a time a pleasant savanna climate. Giraffes, antelopes, and other African savanna animals lived here. So did humans, who left behind pictures of these animals on rocks. In the last few thousand years the Sahara has dried out. The savanna animals retreated south, but some stayed behind on the mountains. Even lions and crocodiles could be found here, until people killed them off earlier this century.

▼ *An insect, not a stone.* In a stony region of the Sahara Desert, the coloring of this preying mantis allows it to hide from enemies and, just as important, from possible prey, including other mantids.

▲ *The European bee-eater* lives in open country and catches insects in the air. It is just one of the birds that North Africa shares with Europe and Asia rather than the rest of Africa. The blue tit, great tit and coal tit are other typically European birds that are found in Morocco and Algeria. The spur-thighed tortoise lives from the Balkans to North Africa. The Mediterranean chameleon lives in Spain and North Africa.

A HUGE BARRIER

Nowadays the Sahara Desert is a huge barrier for life to cross. As a result, many of the species to the north of the Sahara are the same as those of the Middle East or Europe rather than the rest of Africa.

DESERT LIFE

Water is the key to life in deserts. Many animals' bodies are designed to lose as little water as possible. For example, desert beetles have tough water-proof skins. For the camel, when water is not available, it stops sweating. Its body warms up above "normal" temperature, but as it is a big animal it heats slowly. Night comes, and with it the desert cools. So does the camel. Next morning its temperature is a little under normal, then slowly starts to rise.

Birds can fly to water. Some, such as sandgrouse, may go right out into the desert and make long journeys every day to water holes to drink.

▼ ANIMALS OF THE DESERT

The fennec fox is the smallest of all wild dogs. It sleeps in a daytime burrow and emerges at night to hunt insects and small mammals. Its ears help it find prey as well as being useful for losing heat. Several desert rodents, such as the jerboa, can hop fast on their hind legs, using their long tails to balance. Many desert rodents never drink but get the water they need from the seeds they eat. Camels can stand losing a lot of body water. They replace it with a huge drink when they find water.

Fennec fox

Darkling beetle

Skink

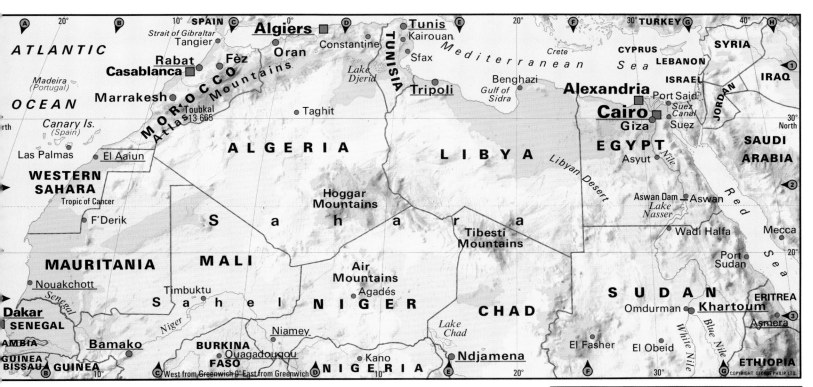

Labels on map include:

ATLANTIC OCEAN, SPAIN, Strait of Gibraltar, Tangier, Algiers, Oran, Constantine, Tunis, Kairouan, Sfax, TUNISIA, Mediterranean Sea, Crete, CYPRUS, TURKEY, SYRIA, LEBANON, ISRAEL, IRAQ, Rabat, Fèz, Casablanca, MOROCCO, Marrakesh, Toubkal 13,665, Taghit, Tripoli, Benghazi, Gulf of Sidra, Alexandria, Port Said, Cairo, Giza, Suez Canal, Suez, JORDAN, SAUDI ARABIA, Madeira (Portugal), Canary Is. (Spain), Las Palmas, El Aaiun, WESTERN SAHARA, Tropic of Cancer, F'Derik, ALGERIA, LIBYA, EGYPT, Asyut, Nile, Libyan Desert, Aswan Dam, Aswan, Lake Nasser, Mecca, Red Sea, Wadi Halfa, Port Sudan, MAURITANIA, MALI, Sahara, Hoggar Mountains, Tibesti Mountains, Nouakchott, Senegal, Sahel, Timbuktu, Air Mountains, Agadés, NIGER, CHAD, SUDAN, Omdurman, Khartoum, ERITREA, Asmera, Dakar, SENEGAL, Niger, Niamey, Lake Chad, El Fasher, El Obeid, White Nile, Blue Nile, GAMBIA, Bamako, BURKINA FASO, Ouagadougou, Kano, Ndjamena, NIGERIA, ETHIOPIA, GUINEA-BISSAU, GUINEA, West from Greenwich, East from Greenwich

MAKING THE MOST OF RAIN

Some desert plants and animals have very tough seeds or eggs that withstand drought and heat. When moistened by a sudden rainstorm they spring to life. The plants grow quickly, and the desert is carpeted with flowers which attract butterflies and other insects.

If temporary puddles and lakes form, tiny shrimps and flies hatch from their eggs and hurry through their life cycle. Toads, too, may start into life and lay eggs. All the activity of these animals' lives must be packed into the time before the desert dries out. It may be years before the next rains.

▲ **THE GREATEST DESERT** in the world touches all the countries of this region. But there are high mountains with cooler conditions in the Hoggar, Tibesti and Aïr massifs, as well as the great Atlas Mountains.

▼ **A common genet** hunts among the acacia trees at the desert's edge. Genets are usually active at night and catch birds, small mammals, reptiles, and insects.

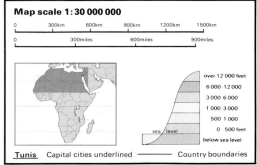

Map scale 1:30 000 000

| 0 | 300km | 600km | 900km | 1200km | 1500km |

| 0 | 300miles | 600miles | 900miles |

over 12 000 feet
6 000–12 000
3 000–6 000
1 000–3 000
500–1 000
0–500 feet
below sea level

Tunis Capital cities underlined ——— Country boundaries

Camel

Desert quail

Jerboa

West and Central Africa

In the forest of this region, you are surrounded by sound, especially at night. You cannot see many insects, but you hear their chirps and whirrs. A chorus of frogs peeps, croaks, and makes other strange sounds. Larger animals call to one another too. In the dark forest they cannot see far, so to keep in touch with others of their kind, they have sound signals that travel well.

One of the most frightening calls is the loud scream of the tree hyrax. It resembles an overgrown guinea pig. But this leaf- and twig-eater is more closely related to elephants. It does not look as though it has the right shape for climbing, but fleshy pads under its feet give it good grip in trees.

SECRET WORLD

Duikers move quietly across the forest floor. These small members of the antelope family feed on fruit and leaves. They live singly or in pairs. Shy and nervous, they take to cover when alarmed. Larger animals live in some forests but may be seldom seen. Giant forest hogs live in thick forest.

Forest elephants, smaller than their savanna relatives, browse the bushes and trees. Pygmy hippos push through the West African forests. One large animal, the okapi, a forest giraffe that is more than 5 feet tall at the shoulders, was not seen by the Europeans until 1901. The thick forest still keeps many mysteries.

SNAKES AND LIZARDS

Many snakes live on the ground, but som are agile and climb in the forest trees:
- Kirtland's tree snake catches birds and lizards in the trees.
- The Gaboon viper is ground living. It grows up to 7 feet long and very fat. Its pattern matches dead leaves on the forest floor. It injects deadly venom from fangs nearly 1.5 inches long.

Chameleons can hold on with four feet ar a tail too. They can change their skin colo This camouflage helps them escape enemi and stalk their food, before shooting o a sticky tongue to catch it. Most kinds chameleon live in Africa.

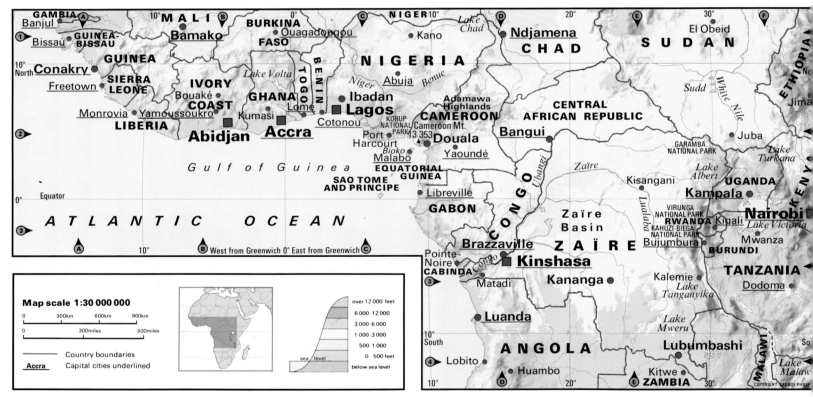

Map scale 1:30 000 000

Country boundaries
Accra Capital cities underlined

over 12 000 feet
6 000·12 000
3 000·6 000
1 000·3 000
500·1 000
0·500 feet
below sea level

◄ **The hooded vulture** is found over much of this region. It is small (only 25 inches long) and usually visits animal carcases after larger vultures. It also picks up small dead animals and scavenges rubbish. Vultures all over Africa do a useful job in removing waste and starting the process of decomposition.

▲ **WEST AND CENTRAL AFRICA** is a hot region, and muc of it has a tropical forest climate. But in some places the natural forest has been removed. Areas like those around the Congo Rive still have large stretches of forest with much wildlife. In the north is the savanna and the southern edge of the Sahara Desert.

▼ MONKEY COUNTRY

The forests of Central Africa are ideal for monkeys. They live high in the trees out of reach of many meat-eaters. They run and jump from branch to branch, some never coming down to the ground. They feed on fruit and leaves. Colobus monkeys, like this red colobus, have special stomachs to deal with their diet of leaves. African monkeys are active by day and sleep at night in the treetops.

REETOP TRAVEL

:ckos are climbing lizards, too. They can ld on, even upside down, using their icky" fingertips. Gliding lizards travel tween the trees by jumping and gliding :h flattened body and tail. Other animals ve the same trick, including scaly-tailed ng squirrels. These rodents live only in ·ica. They have a flap of skin running from ·nt legs to back legs to tail.

Slower are pottos and angwantibos. ese big-eyed, tail-less, distant relatives of ·nkeys move carefully, gripping with hands d feet like chameleons. They stalk insects night. Bush babies, or galagos, are also ations, but they have long tails and are fast nbers and jumpers.

The harnessed bushbuck lives in places ere there is thick cover to hide in. It is well nouflaged in the forest. Only the males have ·ns, which point backward so they do not get ·ght in the dense thickets. Bushbucks pick ·ves, flowers, and pods from the bushes to : but also feed on grass.

▲ **Chimpanzees and their young** live in the forests and on the edges of the savanna. These apes are good at climbing trees but also move from place to place on the ground. They feed mainly on fruits and eat leaves and some meat too. They live in groups. Chimpanzees have a long "childhood," and are nine years old before they are grown up.

▶ **Adult gorillas** are big, heavy apes, and spend most of their time on the forest floor. Females are only half the size of males. Females and young may climb into a tree at night to make a sleeping nest. Gorillas live in big families that move around the forest finding the plant foods that they prefer.

East Africa

This region of mainly natural grassland has the most "big game" in the world. Herds of hundreds of African buffalo are found in the wetter areas. Thousands of zebra, Thomson's gazelle and herds of other plant-eaters dot the plains. Hippopotamuses wade in the lakes and rivers. Black rhinoceroses pick leaves from the bushes. Herds of elephants move quietly to waterholes.

Some huge areas of East Africa are set aside as national parks or reserves. They include the Serengeti, Tsavo, and Masai-Mara. These large areas are needed to give enough space to the herds of big animals, many of which move over hundreds of miles.

RELYING ON OTHERS

When a lion eats a zebra, the food link is obvious. But there are many other kinds of feeding relationships. Some antelopes feed only where the grass has been cropped low enough by other animals. Trees broken down by elephants may provide food for monkeys and antelopes. Elephant dung is food for dung beetles.

Leopard

Lion

▲ *ANIMAL CAMOUFLAGE. The okapi's dark body blends with the forest shadows. The white stripes stand out but cut across its outline. The bongo, too, has stripes that do this and make it hard to see in the broken shadows of the forest. The lion's tawny color helps it blend in with the plain color of the grass it hunts in. The leopard's spots match the dappled leaf shadows among the branches and bushes where it hides.*

GETTING IN LINE

Meat-eaters depend on one another to After lions have made a kill, there is a line scavenge the leftovers. Hyenas, with the bone-cracking jaws, push their way to t front. Jackels, vultures, and smaller anim follow in turn. Vultures circle high in the s hardly moving their wings, until they spo meal below.

Kori bustards strut on the ground, a cranes probe for food. Guinea fowl run flocks through the scrub. Weavers and oth finches live among the trees. Small mamm include mongooses, servals, and caracals, a many kinds of rat and mouse.

BOTTLE TREES

Baobab trees dot the savanna. They ha huge fat trunks that store water, althou they may be hollowed out by anima Baobabs can be home to bats, bush babi and many other animals.

Acacia trees are also common. The stems may have spines 4 inches long, b even this does not deter some animals fr eating their leaves.

◄ *The lion is the biggest of the African hunters. Lions live in groups called prides and work as a team to stalk and catch prey such as wildebeest, zebra, and many smaller animals. A full-grown male lion may weigh 440 pounds, a female 290 pounds. In spite of this weight, they may charge at nearly 40 miles an hour when closing in on prey.*

◄ *Zebras crop the grass* on the savanna. They live in family groups within large herds. They often mix with antelopes and ostriches because the extra eyes and ears make life safer.

Okapi

Bongo

A giraffe feeds on a thorny acacia tree. Its height, its flexible [neck?], and a tongue up to 18 inches long help it pick leaves and bark from trees.

► *EAST AFRICA* is mainly savanna although in the north there is scrub and desert. On the Equator, much is high plateau, which keeps the climate cooler.

Map scale 1:30 000 000

| 0 | 300km | 600km | 900km |
| 0 | 300miles | | 600miles |

———— Country boundaries

Nairobi Capital cities underlined

over 12 000 feet
6 000-12 000
3 000-6 000
1 000-3 000
500-1 000
0-500 feet
below sea level

Southern Africa

Many of the animals of this region are the same types as those which live on savanna elsewhere in Africa – lion, giraffe, impala, reedbuck, and elephant, for example. Others, such as the white-tailed gnu, are just found here. Several kinds of mongoose, like the meerkats which can make a living in the semideserts, are found only here.

PLANT PARADISE

South Africa is rich in plant life, and has many species found nowhere else. They include:
- "old-fashioned" cycads, a type that has survived since the time of the dinosaurs;
- protea shrubs which have huge flowers;
- pretty flowers, such as freesias, that have been taken to gardens all around the world.

ANIMAL CASUALTIES

The southern tip of Africa was settled by farmers who pushed out some wild animals long ago. For example, the springbok antelope once lived in herds so vast that when they migrated it would take several days to trek past any spot. Now comparatively few survive.

◀ *A giant chameleon in a Madagascan forest. Its strong, curled tail can be used for gripping branches. These strange lizards, with eyes that can turn different ways, are still feared by many people.*

▶ *Resting between jumps. Verreaux's sifakas are large lemurs that live in groups up to 12 strong. They are active by day, and travel by jumping from one upright tree trunk to another. They eat fruit and leaves.*

SAVING A RHINO

The white rhino is the bigger of the tw African rhinos. In 1920, only 30 survived southern Africa, so they were put und protection in the Umfolozi Reserve. By 19 there were 2,000. But this was too many the reserve! So some were sent to oth reserves in Africa and zoos around the wor

LEMURS IN MADAGASCAR

This brown mouse lemur is active at night and has big eyes with a shiny reflecting layer at the back. It feeds on fruit, insects, and other small animals. It stores fat in its tail and hibernates in the cool dry months.

It is one of about 30 species of lemur that live in Madagascar. Some are as small as a large mouse. Many are cat-sized. The biggest lemur, the indri, is the size of a large monkey. Lemurs on Madagascar take the place of monkeys in other tropical forests. The oddest lemur is the aye-aye, which has huge eyes, teeth that are good at gnawing into bark, and an incredibly long, thin middle finger with a claw for spearing insects.

ERRIFIC TERMITES!

hroughout the region it is impossible not to otice termites. These insects:

are tiny and blind;
live in colonies;
may have several million in a colony;
feed on dead plants, especially wood;
are very important decomposers in warm countries;
are a major source of food for other animals.

outhern African animals that eat them clude:

the aardwolf – a thin hyena with a special sticky tongue for lapping up termites;
the aardvark – a bare-skinned large animal with long ears. It has big claws to break into termite nests and a long tongue;
the pangolin – with big overlapping "scales" covering its body, large claws, and a long tongue.

URROWS

ll these termite-eaters are active mainly at ght. The Cape pangolin spends the hot urs in a burrow up to 20 feet below ound. Aardvarks, too, make burrows, hich can be more than 32 feet long.

Burrows are useful refuges from danger the heat of the Sun. Many animals use econdhand" aardvark burrows, but the ringhare, a large rodent that jumps on its nd legs, makes its own.

ISLAND REFUGE

Madagascar has been an island for 50 million years. Several types of animals were "marooned" here, and some are now very different to African animals. For example, there are boas, as in South America, but not pythons as in Africa. Special types of mammal have developed, such as lemurs, and tenrecs – spiny-skinned insect-eaters. And there are three special meat-eaters related to mongooses: the falanouc, the fanaloka, and the fossa.

▼ *Jackass penguins* on a rocky shore near the Cape of Good Hope. They get their name from the braying call they make. These penguins breed on islands off the South African coast. Then they swim out to sea to catch fish such as anchovies. A cold ocean current, the Benguela Current, brings cool water from the Antarctic to southern Africa. It also brings much plankton, and so the seas can support many fish.

◄ *High plateau* covers much of southern Africa. Here the vegetation is usually savanna, or veld. On the east coast there are forested areas, and these are also found in the valleys of big rivers such as the Zambezi and Limpopo. In the west the climate is drier. The coastal Namib Desert gives its name to Namibia, and the Kalahari Desert takes up much of Botswana and stretches into Namibia and South Africa.

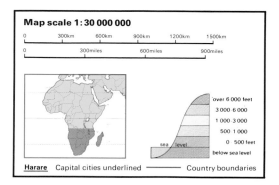

Map scale 1:30 000 000

Harare Capital cities underlined ——— Country boundaries

AUSTRALIA

Everyone knows the kangaroos of Australia, but they are only one of the many kinds of pouched mammal that live here. Phalangers, or possums, climb trees and feed on fruit, leaves, or insects. Some, the gliders, have a parachute of skin between their legs and glide from tree to tree. Much bigger, and slower moving, are koalas, which feed on eucalyptus leaves. Wombats live on and under ground and feed on roots.

MARSUPIALS

Marsupials are primitive mammals. They give birth to half-developed young which grow into fully developed babies in the pouch. There are marsupial equivalents to many of the more advanced mammals on other continents (see pages 18–19). For example, there is a marsupial mole and a marsupial anteater. Pouched "mice" capture insects for food.

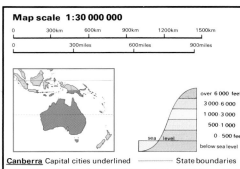

Map scale 1:30 000 000

| 0 | 300km | 600km | 900km | 1200km | 1500km |

| 0 | 300miles | 600miles | 900miles |

over 6 000 feet
3 000·6 000
1 000·3 000
500·1 000
0·500 feet
sea level
below sea level

Canberra Capital cities underlined   ——— State boundaries

STAMP MESSAGE
Australia has plenty of wildlife to show on its stamps. They are good for publicizing species in danger, such as the hairy-nosed wombat.

▼ *AUSTRALIA* has a dry middle where
d kangaroos and other animals live in the
en country. In the north there is lush tropical
rest, with kangaroos, gliders, and other
ssums in it. Crocodiles live in the northern
ers. The Great Barrier Reef off the east
ast is the largest coral reef in the world.
has 300 kinds of coral, plus fish of all
apes and sizes, starfish, and octopuses.
is one of the richest habitats on Earth.

▲ *The eastern gray kangaroo* moves
slowly on all fours when it is grazing. But if
it is frightened and in a hurry, it hops on its
hind legs at speeds up to 53 miles an hour.

► *A red-eyed tree frog* balances on a rain
forest twig. Round pads on the ends of
its fingers and toes help it grip. In Australia
and New Guinea there are 150 different
tree frog species, many brightly colored.

OTHER ODDITIES

Australia is the only continent where there are more venomous snakes than harmless. Most of them belong to the cobra family. They include the tiger snake, one of the most deadly of all snakes. There are also several kinds of python.

There are many parrots in Australia. It is the home of cockatoos, with crests on their heads. Some, such as the galah, are farm pests. Wild budgerigars live in the dry outback in large flocks.

SURVIVING DROUGHT

Most of inland Australia is desert. Many animals, such as the knob-tailed gecko, survive by burrowing. The echidna has big claws and can dig deep. The water-holding frog takes in water and stores it in its bladder until the rains come again.

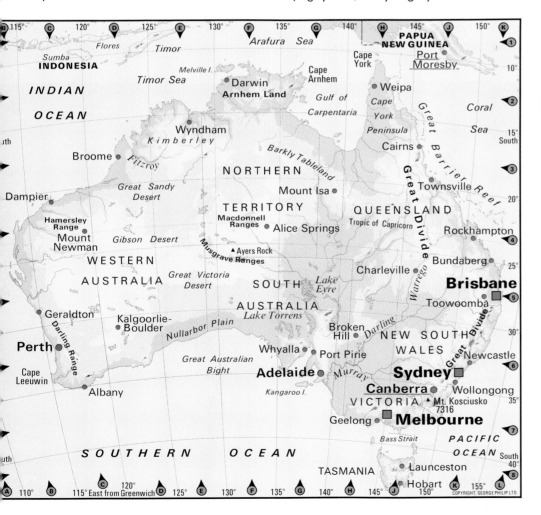

Pacific Islands

Many of the islands of the Pacific Ocean have developed their own kinds of wildlife. That of New Guinea is similar to Australia; there are marsupials and cockatoos as well as the spectacular birds of paradise. The males have very showy feathers and strange courtship dances.

KINGDOM OF BIRDS

New Zealand is very different. It has been separate from the rest of the world since before the mammals evolved. Before settlers arrived, only two species of mammal reached here, both of them bats. About 30 kinds of reptile were native, most of them lizards of the skink and gecko families. There were three kinds of frog. But most of the backboned animals were birds.

The kiwi is the national bird. It cannot fly and has rather hair-like feathers. Its vision is poor, but it has a long sensitive beak which it uses to probe for worms at night. It lays the biggest egg for its size of any bird. In New Zealand, birds took over the ways of life of mammals in other places.

NO MOA

Several kinds of larger flightless bird, called moas, some bigger than ostriches, used to live in New Zealand. But they were killed off after the Maori people settled the country.

The same sad story of disappearance can be told of island species all over the world. The animals cannot withstand hunting, interference with their habitat, and the introduction of animals from outside. These new animals may attack them or eat the foods that they need to survive.

UNIQUE HAWAII

The Hawaiian islands in the middle of the Pacific were reached by few animals. But those that did arrive were able to evolve into all kinds of ways of life. The number of species grew so that Hawaii now has 1,000 snails found nowhere else and four times as many insects.

When Captain Cook sailed here in 1778 there were 70 special Hawaiian land birds, including 28 kinds of honeycreepers with different beaks for different kinds of food.

TURTLE BEACH
A loggerhead turtle returns to the sea after laying her eggs. Turtles use sandy beaches on many of the islands in this region for their nests. This turtle has a tag on its flipper. People are trying to find out more about its movements. Many turtle species are becoming rarer because too many eggs have been collected for food.

▲ **Sooty terns** at a breeding colony. These fish-eating birds live in the tropical seas and nest on many Pacific islands. Outside the breeding season they may be seen at sea far from land, sometimes following ships at night.

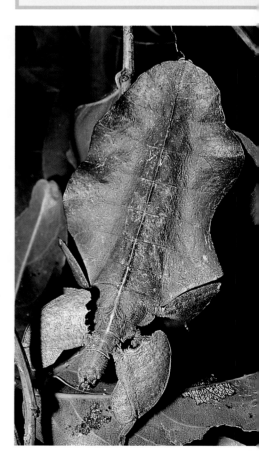

► **This leaf insect** is just the right color and shape to resemble a dead leaf and so be ignored by a predator. It lives in New Guinea. Other kinds are green, like new leaves, or are blotched brown, like diseased leaves.

HE SEAS AND CORAL REEFS

he seas around the islands contain sharks,
anta rays, turtles, and other animals. Many
lands are fringed with coral, giving a home
o fish of all shapes and sizes and small
nimals, from worms to sea urchins.

The seas also provide food for birds.
Many nest on safe island beaches. Noddies,
ed-footed boobies, and terns nest on
lands in the tropical Pacific.

▲ **THE PACIFIC ISLANDS** are just dots in
the ocean. Groups of islands are separated by
thousands of miles of sea. Only animals that
are good travelers or have been blown there
by chance are likely to colonize them, unless
people have taken them there.

► **NEW ZEALAND** consists of two main
islands. Before people arrived, there were
almost no mammals, but many special birds.

Grizzlies, pronghorns, beavers, skunks, rattlesnakes, and coyotes: These are among the best-known animals of North America.

Each of these creatures prefers to live in a different kind of habitat. But in North America this presents no problem. There is almost every kind of habitat you can think of, from the freezing wilderness regions of northern Canada to the hot rain forests of Central America. In between are cool forests, warm grasslands, arid deserts, and steamy wetlands. There is also an enormous variety of plants:

- Maple trees in Canada.
- Giant redwoods and sequoias in California.
- Yuccas in the western deserts.
- Mangroves in Florida.

HIGHLANDS

High mountains run all the way down the western side of the continent from Alaska to Central America. They are known as the Cordilleras. The main chain is the Rocky Mountains, or Rockies. Evergreen forests of fir, spruce, and pine cover much of the mountain slopes. They are the home of the grizzly bear, black bear, and various deer.

▲ A bull moose drinking in a mountain stream in northern Canada. It sports a fresh set of antlers, with some of the peeled-off velvet on either side of its head. The moose is bulkier than other deer.

Wet and Wild

Preserving Wetlands
1934 1984
USA 20c

Canada 57

SMOKEY

USA 20c

Washington
1889

USA 25

Canada 76

These stamps feature:
- the deadly killer whale;
- the magnificent grizzly bear;
- the smaller American black bear;
- ducks and wetlands;
- the wilds of Washington State.

NORTHERN FOREST

The main forest region on the continent, however, is the great boreal (northern) conifer forest. It sweeps in a broad band from Alaska to Newfoundland. Spruce and pine are the main tree species. The boreal forest is the home of the caribou, the moose, the black bear, and the beaver.

PLAINS AND DESERTS

In the middle of the continent, a vast lowland area stretches from the Rockies to the low Appalachian mountain chain in the east. The higher, drier western part of the region makes up the Great Plains, a vast belt of temperate grassland, or prairie. Last century the prairie teemed with huge herds of buffalo and pronghorn, but settlers hunted the herds nearly to extinction. There are scattered patches of tropical grassland, or savanna, in the central United States.

North America's main deserts are in the southwest, in California, Arizona, and Mexico. There, only one or two inches of rain fall every year. Various kinds of cactus are the main plant life, while animals include snakes, lizards, and scorpions.

▲ **A gopher snake** of the Arizona desert poised ready to strike. It may bite but is not poisonous. It is a constrictor, which means that it kills by coiling its body around prey and squeezing the animal to death. Similar snakes called bull snakes or pine snakes are found widely throughout the US.

▲ **The colorful purple gallinule** can be found in freshwater wetlands throughout the southern United States. It is also called water hen or sultana. With its long, thin toes, it can run swiftly across lily pads and other floating vegetation. Purple gallinules have a white, fleshy plate on the head.

NORTH AMERICAN RECORDS
North America has the world's:
- Largest carnivore, the polar bear – up to 10 feet long.
- Longest migrator, the arctic tern. It migrates 9,000 miles to the Antarctic and returns the next year.
- Biggest living thing, the giant sequoia tree, named General Sherman – 266 feet tall, 82 feet in girth.
- Smallest bird, the bee hummingbird of Cuba – 0.2 inches long.
- Rarest bird of prey, the California condor – less than 30 captive birds.

▲ **NORTH AMERICA** *is a land of great contrasts. It has vast mountainous regions in the west and great open plains to the east. It experiences bitter cold in the north, yet tropical heat in the south. It has every habitat and a wealth of wildlife, from mouse to mountain lion, from cactus to giant redwood.*

Canada and Alaska

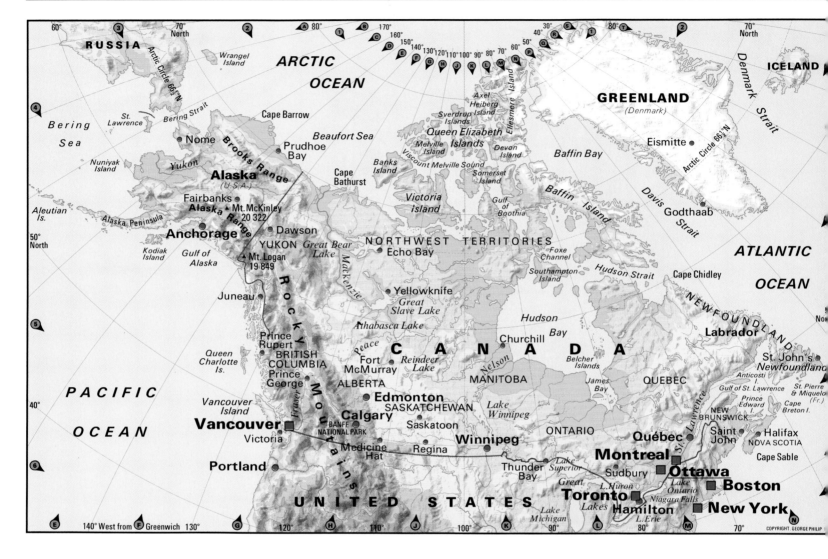

Canada and Alaska have some of the biggest expanses of wilderness left on Earth. Because of the harsh climate over much of the region, few people live there, and there is little industrial development. This makes it a good place for wildlife.

There are two main natural habitats in North America:
• Tundra: bleak, treeless land, lying mainly within the Arctic Circle.
• Boreal forest: a broad expanse of conifer forest, part of a belt that girdles northern regions of the world.

There are also large expanses of open grasslands, or prairie, further south and mountains in the west. These regions have similar wildlife to the prairies and mountains of the western states (see pages 62 and 63).

TUNDRA LIFE

It is too cold on the tundra for tall trees to survive. The most successful plants are grasses such as cotton grass and small bushes such as crowberries.

For much of the year the tundra is frozen. It thaws in early summer, but the ground remains frozen deep down. The landscape becomes boggy because the water cannot drain away. For just a few weeks the Sun shines warmly. Tundra plants have to shoot, flower, and set seed rapidly before the temperature starts to drop in early fall.

As the grass starts growing, great herds of caribou migrate to the tundra from the conifer forests. Wolves and black bears follow the caribou, preying on their young and on other small mammals.

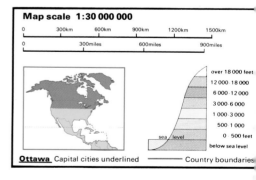

▲ **THE COUNTRY OF CANADA**
and the American state of Alaska make up more than half of North America. Much of the region is quite barren and lies inside the Arctic Circle. The Rocky Mountains form a formidable barrier in the west. Most of the people live in the south.

An American black bear rears up
its hind legs to get a better view of the
photographer. Standing upright like this, it is
taller than a man. Black bears roam in most
forest areas. Shortage of food may drive them
to scavenge at waste dumps on camp sites.

Winter coat

Summer coat

▲ *The arctic hare* lives in the far north,
where summers are short and winters are
long and snowy. It has a brownish coat in
summer, but this changes to white in winter
to blend in with the snow.

▲ *The arctic fox* also changes its coat
from summer to winter. Here in winter,
its coat is pure white. This gives it good
camouflage in the snow so that it can
creep up on its prey without being seen.

SUMMER MIGRANTS

The snowy owl lives all year in the tundra,
preying mainly on small animals. It is joined
in summer by a host of migrant birds,
particularly geese. Vast flocks of snow,
Canada and white-fronted geese descend on
the tundra to breed. They head back south
again in the fall.

THE BOREAL FORESTS

Conifers, such as spruce, are the main trees
in the boreal forest region. Their needle-like
leaves do not lose heat as quickly as broad
leaves. Also, the conical shape of the conifer
makes it shed snow from its branches easily.

The biggest animals in the conifer forests
are deer and bears. They include the moose,
the caribou (called reindeer in Europe), and
the wapiti. American black bears are also
common, although their color may also be
blue, brown, and even white! In the west
of the region grizzly bears are also found,
particularly on the higher ground. When
rearing up, an adult male grizzly stands more
than 10 feet tall.

HUNTING AND TRAPPING

The boreal forests also teem with much
smaller animals that have long been hunted
and trapped for their fur or skin. They
include the lynx, marten, mink, beaver, and
muskrat. Some species, such as the lynx, are
now getting scarce.

Beavers and muskrats live around the
streams and lakes. Beavers dam streams to
create deeper water for their lodge.

▼ *A dense flock of blue geese* migrating
north over Canada. They are on their way to
their summer breeding grounds in the Arctic.
The blue goose, which has bluish-grey and
white plumage, is a variety of snow goose.
During the brief Arctic summer, blue geese
nest on the tundra. In the fall, before the
snows return, the geese wing their way back
to the US Gulf coast. They fly together in
flocks of thousands of birds.

Western United States

The western US is a region of mountains, prairie, scrub, and desert. There is even a small area of rain forest on the northwest coast. It is a temperate rain forest, home of the giant redwood and sequoia trees.

The main mountain ranges are the Rocky Mountains and, further west, the Sierra Nevada (Snowy Mountains). Wild sheep called bighorns live in the highest regions.

CAT COUNTRY

The mountains and foothills are also the stalking ground for two of the continent's wild cats. Biggest is the puma, or cougar, also known as the mountain lion. The favorite prey of this beautiful creature is deer. The other cat is the bobcat, a shy creature about twice the size of the domestic cat. It hunts and eats mainly rodents.

WHERE THE BUFFALO ROAM

East of the Rockies are the Great Plains. This is a vast expanse of temperate grassland. It was once the home of very large herds of buffalo, or bison. But only a few small herds now remain, mostly in national parks.

▼ *The buffalo, or American bison, is a huge animal, standing up to 6.5 feet tall at the shoulders. It has a woolly mane over the head and shoulders. In winter it grows a thick coat over most of its body to keep it warm.*

The pronghorn has suffered a similar fate. It is a deer-like animal noted for its speed. It is preyed on by bobcats and the wild dogs of the prairie, coyotes. Coyotes also prey on prairie dogs. These rodents live together underground in large "towns," or coteries.

SCRUB AND DESERT

In the southwest there is scant rainfall and vast areas of scrub and desert. In California this area is called the chaparral. Here rodents like kangaroo rats are preyed on by deadly snakes, such as sidewinders and rattlesnakes.

Fleet-footed residents include the bird called the roadrunner and the antelope jackrabbit. This rabbit has remarkably big ears, which allow it to lose body heat quickly.

Plant life in the arid lands is sparse, mainly tussock grass, yuccas, and cacti. Two of the most common cacti are:
- The prickly pear cactus, which has flat, oval-shaped stems and edible fruit.
- The saguaro cactus, which has long stems and may grow to 50 feet tall.

Cacti are well adapted to desert life, having no leaves and a stem that retains water. They have spines to protect them from animals. Many have exquisite flowers.

▲ *The yucca is a common plant in the arid lands of the southwestern US. It is an evergreen, with a short stem and stiff, spiky leaves. The flowers are bell-shaped and grow on stems that rise from the leaf clusters.*

▼ *The desert iguana is a small lizard of western desert regions. At the hottest times of the day, it seeks shade or burrows just below the surface to escape the Sun's heat.*

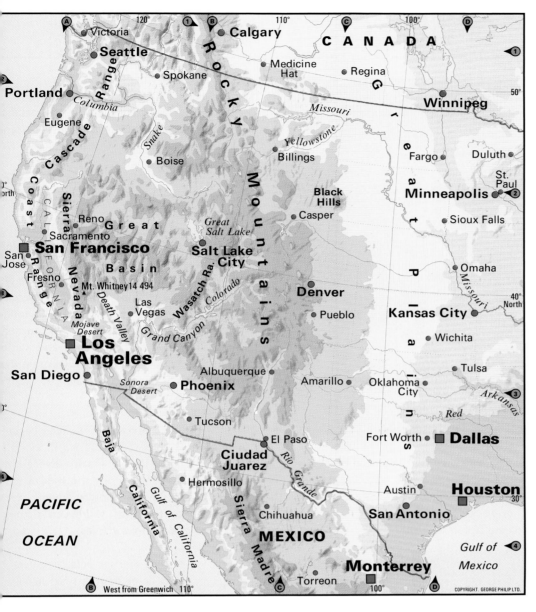

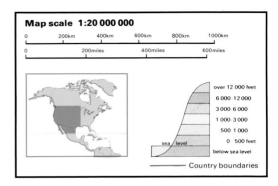

Map scale 1:20 000 000

over 12 000 feet
6 000-12 000
3 000-6 000
1 000-3 000
500-1 000
sea level   0-500 feet
below sea level
— Country boundaries

◄ **THE WESTERN US** has spectacular scenery. Running north-south are the rugged Rocky Mountains. Nearer the coast is the lower Sierra Nevada range. In the south is a vast hot, dry region that includes the Mojave and Sonora deserts and Death Valley, one of the hottest places on Earth.

▲ **On guard**. Even as it eats, a prairie dog remains watchful. If it spots an intruder, it calls out a warning to other animals so that they can run into their burrows. Prairie dogs live on the prairies and mountain plains.

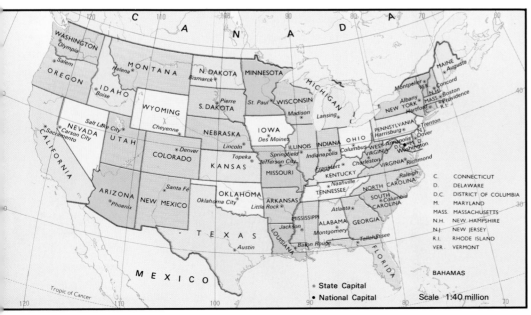

◄ **STATES OF THE US** and their capital cities. This map shows only 48 of the 50 states. The other two are Alaska, west of Canada, and Hawaii, over 1,850 miles away in the Pacific Ocean. The eastern states were the first to be settled and much of the population now lives there. The big cities, such as New York and Washington, are centers for business and government. In other parts of the country, farming, mining, manufacturing, and tourism are important industries. All these activities conflict with wildlife.

Eastern United States

In the north, a series of huge freshwater lakes straddles the border with Canada. Called the Great Lakes, they are now connected by canals to each other and to the St. Lawrence River.

Some of the lakes suffer badly from pollution, but they are still the home of abundant wildlife. Fish and eels swim in the waters, which attract a rich variety of bird life, from ducks and waders to herring gulls and terns. The area is also an important wintering ground for migrants.

MARVELOUS MONARCHS

During the summer millions of monarch butterflies breed around the Great Lakes. But when winter approaches they fly south to warmer places. They fly as far as Florida and Mexico, making journeys of up to 1,850 miles. In the spring, the butterflies or their offspring head back north, to their Great Lakes breeding grounds.

▲ **The mischievous face of a common raccoon.** *Raccoons have a fox-like face with a black mask. Their tail is bushy and ringed. They quickly adapt to new surroundings and can eat almost anything.*

▼ **An American alligator** *pokes its snout out of the undergrowth in the Everglades in Florida. Alligators are now protected and are found in large numbers throughout the wetlands in the south of the region.*

OLD MAN RIVER

In the east, the Great Plains give way to lowland region of generally higher rainfal This area is drained by the Missouri an Mississippi rivers and their tributaries. Th whole region has productive farmland fo crops and livestock. In the south, where th climate is warm, subtropical crops such a cotton are grown.

The streams all along the Mississipp flood plain are home to mammals like mink otter, muskrats, and many birds. In th south, toward the Mississippi delta, there ar vast hot, humid swamps, where the America alligator thrives. Alligators are to be foun throughout the marshlands of the souther states. They feed on fish, snakes, and turtle and may attack dogs and cattle. It is said tha they can run as fast as a human!

GRASSY WATERS

One of the most extensive wetland region in the whole of North America is found i the southeast. It is the Florida Everglade: called "Grassy Waters" by the Indians. It i really a vast, shallow, slowly flowing rive It drains into the Gulf of Mexico throug coastal thickets of mangroves.

▼ **FOUR BIRDS OF PREY**
of the region:
- The common black hawk, which feeds on frogs and fish.
- The magnificent golden eagle. The span of its wings can reach over 6.5 feet. It is quite rare.
- The American bald eagle gets its name from its white head, which makes it look bald. It is the national bird of the US.
- The gyrfalcon usually lives in the far north. It is the biggest member of the falcon family.

Common black hawk

Golden eagle

Killer whales, or orcas, swimming in [sou]thern waters. They are closely related [to] dolphins but are much bigger. Hunting [in p]acks, they are ferocious predators.

THE EASTERN UNITED STATES

[is r]elatively flat. The Great Plains cover a vast [are]a in the west. In the east is a low mountain [ran]ge, the Appalachians. In the far south the [sw]ampy Everglades is a haven for wildlife.

Map scale   1:20 000 000

200km	400km	600km	800km	1000km

200miles	400miles	600miles

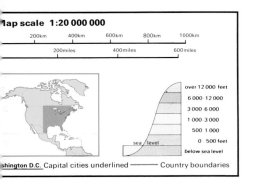

over 12 000 feet
6 000 - 12 000
3 000 - 6 000
1 000 - 3 000
500 - 1 000
0   500 feet
sea level
below sea level

[Wa]shington D.C. Capital cities underlined ——— Country boundaries

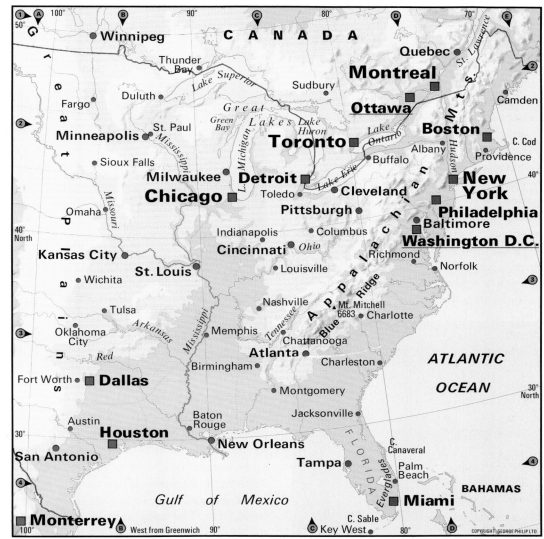

Bald eagle

Gyrfalcon

LIFE IN THE SWAMPS

Mangroves are well adapted to live in salty tidal waters. They send down roots from their trunk and branches, which are able to take in air. In this way the tree can "breathe" when its ground roots are covered by sea.

The Everglades has rich wildlife. As well as alligators, there are crocodiles. Among the rare mammals are the Florida panther — a local name for the puma — and the manatee. The manatee, or sea cow, is an entirely aquatic creature. But it is the bird life of the Everglades that is really outstanding and includes such species as the:

- Bald eagle and osprey;
- Roseate spoonbill and flamingos;
- Great white heron and egrets;
- Everglades kite and peregrine falcon;
- Brown pelican and sandhill crane;
- Mangrove cuckoo and Cape Sable sparrow;
- Wood stork and anhinga.

Central America and West Indies

Central America bridges the gap between the great North and South American continents. The interior is mountainous. The biggest chain is the Sierra Madre. Some of its peaks are volcanoes, including the famous Popocatepetl (Smoking Mountain).

Much of northern Mexico is desert, a continuation of the Arizona desert in the United States. Baja California is mostly desert too. The deserts boast a great variety of cacti, including the organ-pipe cactus, which looks rather like a candelabra, and the tall saguaro cactus. Agaves, or century plants, are also common.

SWEET-TOOTHED SUCKERS

The flowers of saguaro cacti and century plants provide an unlikely source of food for a bat, the Mexican long-nosed bat. It is a nectar-eater, with a long tongue to thrust deep inside the flowers.

In the same family is the biggest New World bat, the false vampire bat. It and the true vampire bats, which suck blood from animals, are found throughout most of South America.

▲ *A white peacock butterfly with wings outstretched alights on a leaf in a Mexican forest. Notice the dark eyespots on its pale wings. White peacocks can be found throughout Central America. Other peacocks are more brilliantly colored and more boldly marked. Peacocks are found throughout the world and form part of the largest group of true butterflies, which has more than 6,000 members. This group also includes the well-known admirals and tortoiseshells.*

▲ **The agouti** *lives in the tropical rain forests of Panama. This rodent feeds on fruit and buries any surplus to eat later, so helping to spread the seeds.*

▶ **MEXICO** *is by far the largest country in the region. It is many times bigger and has considerably more people than all the other countries put together. Central America has a backbone range of high mountains, with flat plains along the coasts. In southern Mexico and the other countries, the coastal plains have heavy rainfall. Much of this coastal region is covered with thick rain forest.*

RÉPUBLIQUE D'HAÏTI

COLORFUL ISLANDER

The pink-feathered roseate spoonbill is featured on this stamp from the Caribbean country of Haiti. It is one of the most colorful birds found in Haiti. It is also found in estuaries and lakes throughout the region. Roseate spoonbills feed on fish and crustaceans, which they catch with their spoon-like bills.

HE CHEWING GUM TREE

ne coastal plains on either side of the terior mountains in southern Mexico and e rest of Central America get plenty of in. They are covered with thick rain forest valuable hardwoods, such as mahogany, ony, and rosewood. Another useful tree hich grows there is the sapodilla, from hich chicle is produced. This is made into ewing gum.

The animal life in the forest largely irrors that of the South American rain rests. It includes parrots and tree frogs, akes, armadillos and anteaters, sloths and ossums, and jaguars.

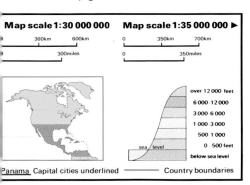

Map scale 1:30 000 000   Map scale 1:35 000 000 ▶

over 12 000 feet
6 000 - 12 000
3 000 - 6 000
1 000 - 3 000
500 - 1 000
0 - 500 feet
below sea level

Panama Capital cities underlined ——— Country boundaries

TROPICAL ISLANDS.

Almost all of the any islands in the West Indies lie within the pics. The temperature remains quite high roughout most of the year, and plenty of rain lls. Most of the islands have areas of thick rest and lush vegetation, and some have high untains. Large amounts of land have been eared for agriculture. Sugar cane, bananas, d tobacco are widely grown.

▲ *Blue-footed boobies are common along the Pacific coast of Central America. They get their name because they seem stupid, allowing themselves to be easily caught by predators and people.*

A MEETING PLACE

These animals are examples of species that evolved in South America when it was a separate continent. They began moving northward when it linked up with North America some 3 million years ago. Central America is thus a mixing ground for species from each continent. Its mountains, for example, are the home of both the North American puma and the South American jaguar, cats with a similar lifestyle.

PALMS AND SANDY BEACHES

Most of the scattered islands in the Caribbean, or West Indies, are low-lying. But the larger ones, particularly Hispaniola, have highlands inland. The islands are usually circled with coral reefs and edged with sandy beaches, coconut palm trees, and mangrove thickets. Water animals include numerous sea turtles and manatees, or sea cows. Parrots abound in the trees of the island's tropical forests: Some species are restricted to certain islands. The spectacular long-billed toucan can also be found.

Perhaps the rarest creature in the islands is the solenodon, found only in Cuba and Hispaniola. It is an insect-eater, rather like a shrew only much bigger.

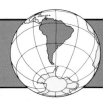

▲ Shaped like a triangle, South America has a varied landscape and range of climates. Most of the land is relatively flat, except for the Andes Mountains in the west. This range contains many very high peaks that are permanently covered in snow. The climate changes from equatorial in the north to cold temperate in the south and alpine in the Andes. The southern tip of the continent is closer to Antarctica than any other landmass.

uth America has a richer variety of ldlife than any other continent. About quarter of all known kinds of animals live ere. In its jungles and tropical forests e the world's smallest monkey, the biggest ake, and tadpoles bigger than frogs. In rivers swim menacing crocodiles, vicious ranhas, and electric eels. Vampire bats, isonous tree frogs, large and small dents, camel-like grazers, and animals that ise their young in pouches are all to be und in different parts of this fascinating ntinent.

OUNTAINS, JUNGLES, PLAINS

ost of South America is quite flat, but along e western coast runs one of the highest ountain ranges in the world. It is the Andes ountain range. East of the Andes is the nazon Basin, the biggest river basin the orld. It is a huge area of jungle, rain forest, d swamp, drained by the River Amazon, e longest river in the Americas.

South of the rain forests, which lie mainly Brazil, comes a scrubland area called the ran Chaco. South of this is a vast region of mperate grassland known as the pampas. is the equivalent of the prairies of orth America.

The narrow coastal plain between the des and the Pacific Ocean includes one of e driest places on Earth – the Atacama esert in Chile. In some parts of it rain has t fallen for over 400 years!

BIG, SMALL, SLOW
South America has the world's:
- Second longest river, the Amazon – 4,007 miles long.
- Most poisonous frog, the golden poison-dart frog of Colombia. It has enough poison to kill up to 1,500 people.
- Biggest snake, the anaconda – up to 33 feet long.
- Biggest spider, the goliath bird-eating spider – 11 inches.
- Smallest monkey, the pygmy marmoset – under 8 inches long and 7 ounces in weight.
- Slowest mammal, the three-toed sloth – speed 6.5 feet a minute.
- Biggest rodent, the capybara – up to 4.5 feet in length.

▲ **Tent-builders.** *This bat lives in the tropical rain forests. It is one of the tent-building bats. These clever creatures bite through the stem of a large leaf so that it folds over to make a "tent." This gives them shelter from the heavy rain that falls almost every day in the forests.*

▼ **Dense jungle in eastern Peru.** *The big tree here thrusts its topmost branches up to 130 feet above the ground to reach the sunlight. The structures at the base of the tree trunk are known as buttresses. They give the tall tree extra support.*

DOWN IN THE JUNGLE
The largest numbers of different kinds of animals and plants live in the Amazon Basin. Much of the rain forest region, or *selvas*, remains unexplored. It almost certainly contains many species of plants and animals that are still to be discovered. We may never know what they are because the Amazonian rain forests are being devastated by logging and "slash and burn" agriculture.

A GRIPPING TAIL
Many South American species are distinctly different from those on other continents. For example, several of the monkeys have something that sets them apart from the monkeys of Africa. They have a prehensile tail, which they wrap around a branch to swing from and for added support.

▲ **Giant coots** *gather together on a lake in Lauca National Park in Chile. The lake is situated over 13,000 feet high in the Andes mountain range. The snow-covered peak in the distance is a volcano.*

PLENTY OPOSSUMS
The main grazers of the pampas are quite unlike the pronghorn and buffalo that graze the American prairie. They are camel-like creatures and various rodents related to that popular pet the guinea pig.

Indeed, guinea pig-like animals are almost everywhere. So are opossums. These are marsupials, animals whose females raise their young in a pouch, or fold of skin on their belly. Most opossums have a prehensile tail. Australasia is the only other region of the world where marsupials are found (see pages 54 and 55).

Andean South America

The great Andes mountain chain snakes in an elongated S-shape all the way down the west coast of South America. The range has permanent snow-capped peaks, high plateaus, rocky cliffs, and rolling foothills. Up on the plateaus are cold, windswept grasslands and many lakes, large and small. Biggest by far is Lake Titicaca, which straddles the Peru-Bolivia border. The lower slopes of the Andes are heavily forested.

MOUNTAIN ANIMALS

Because of the harsh climate, relatively few animals live at the highest altitudes. But lower down, the grassy plateaus and forest regions are home for some interesting wildlife. The puma, or mountain lion, is a major predator, as it is throughout the Americas. The outstanding bird of prey is the majestic Andean condor, one of the New World vultures. It is still found in some numbers, unlike the California condor, which is thought to be extinct in the wild.

In the northern Andes lives the only kind of bear on the continent, the spectacled bear. It has a dark, shaggy coat and gets its name from the white markings around the eyes. It is mainly a fruit-eater, although it may also prey on young deer and vicuñas.

▶ *THE ANDES MOUNTAINS* *run along the whole western side of South America. The highest peaks rise above 19,500 feet and are snow-covered all year. The Andes also have several active volcanoes, such as Cotopaxi in Ecuador. The main headstreams of the great Amazon, Parana and Orinoco rivers rise in the eastern Andes. To the west is a narrow coastal plain, much of which has a very dry climate. It is driest in the Atacama Desert in Chile.*

▶ *High up in the Andes, vicuñas search for grass to eat. These small members of the camel family live between 11,500 and 15,500 feet above sea level. They are still hunted for their meat and furry coat.*

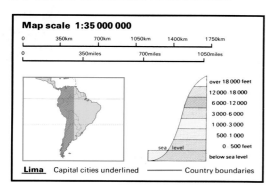

Map scale 1:35 000 000

Lima   Capital cities underlined   ———— Country boundaries

over 18 000 feet
12 000-18 000
6 000-12 000
3 000-6 000
1 000-3 000
500-1 000
0-500 feet
below sea level

ENCHANTED ISLES

This is an old name for the Galapagos Islands in the Pacific. They are famed for their distinctive wildlife, such as giant tortoises, land iguanas and finches. His study of Galapagos wildlife in the 1830s helped the great English naturalist Charles Darwin work out his now celebrated ideas and theory of natural selection and evolution of plants and animals (see page 19).

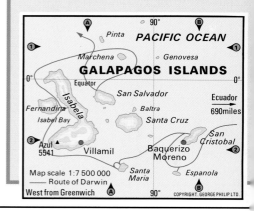

Map scale 1:7 500 000
——— Route of Darwin
West from Greenwich

◄ **Colorful but deadly.** *This coral snake is found in the scrubland and deserts of the region. It is quite small, measuring only about 30 inches long, but its bite is deadly and can kill a human.*

► **A mountain viscacha mother** *suckling her young up in the Andes. Mountain viscachas are rodents. Like chinchillas, they have a soft, furry coat. Their numbers have been greatly reduced by hunting.*

FINE WOOL

Two other lamoids have been domesticated and are not found in the wild. They are the llama and the alpaca. The llama is kept as a pack animal, while the alpaca is raised for its fine wool used to make clothing.

CUDDLY CAVIES

Cavies (guinea pigs) and related rodents thrive throughout South America. Several species make their home on the high plateaus and slopes of the Andes.

One is the chinchilla. It is about half the size of a rabbit, with a fine furry coat, big ears and a long bushy tail. It was once hunted almost to extinction because its coat is highly prized. Now it is bred commercially in captivity for its fur.

RELATED RODENTS

The mountain viscacha also inhabits the Andes region. It is closely related to the chinchilla, but has a heavier body and coarser fur. A different species, called the Plains viscacha, lives in lowland regions.

Among other cavy-like rodents are the small chinchilla rat and the tuco-tuco. The chinchilla rat is sometimes hunted for its soft fur. The stocky tuco-tuco is named for its call. It lives underground and feeds on plant bulbs and roots.

SPITTING CAMELS

The vicuña is a small grazing animal closely related to the camel. It is one of the four cameloids, or lamoids, of South America. Unlike the camel, these animals have no hump. They have a slender body, long legs and neck, and a short tail. When they get annoyed, they spit!

The vicuña lives on the high plateaus of the Andes, up to 15,500 feet. The foothills of the mountains are preferred by its larger relative, the guanaco.

◄ **Guanacos roam** *among the cacti in the Atacama Desert in Chile. They also make their home in the foothills of the Andes and on the South American plains, or pampas. The guanaco is the ancestor of the llama.*

▼ **A thorny question** *– a prickly branch on a rain forest tree in Venezuela? No, the small prickles are a cluster of insects often called treehoppers. You can see how they got their other name – thorn bugs.*

Amazonian South America

The Amazon River is fed by at least a thousand feed rivers, or tributaries. Most of them rise in the Andes. The river basin they drain covers an area nearly the size of Australia. The Amazon Basin straddles the Equator, and the climate is always hot, wet, and humid. This results in the selvas, a vast region of rain forest that has no equal in any other part of the world.

North and south of the Amazon Basin, the climate gradually changes to give distinct wet and dry seasons. This produces a landscape of deciduous woodlands and open grassland, or savanna. In Venezuela and Colombia the savanna becomes extensive in the Orinoco River Basin, where it is called the llanos (plains).

RUBBER AND ORCHIDS

Some 2,500 species of trees grow in the rain forests. They include valuable hardwoods like the jarana and matamata, and the Brazil nut tree. Many palm trees flourish, yielding nuts and oil. Some are tapped for their sap. The sap of *Hevea brasiliensis* yields rubber. It is the ancestor of the rubber trees now cultivated in plantations worldwide.

Throughout the forests, thick vines called lianas twine around the tree trunks. The trees also support many epiphytes, or air plants. They grow in tree crevices and take moisture directly from the air. Among them are beautiful orchids and spiky-leaved bromeliads, plants related to the pineapple.

ANTS WITH UMBRELLAS!

Ants galore can be seen in the rain forests of the Amazon Basin. Some ants bite leaves into pieces and walk about with them over their heads, apparently using them as umbrellas. They are called parasol ants.

But these leaf-cutting ants are not trying to keep off the rain! They are taking bits of leaf back to their nest. Back in the nest they place the bits in a special "garden" and grow a fungus on them. This produces little heads that the ants feed on.

CHATTERING MONKEYS

The forests are exceedingly noisy. Parrots of every hue screech and squawk up in the canopy, and groups of monkeys chatter and squabble incessantly. There are two families of monkeys in these forests: tamarins and marmosets, and capuchins.

Tamarins and marmosets are all small monkeys, with a fine silky coat. Some have a long mane or a moustache. One of the most striking monkeys is the golden lion tamarin; it is also one of the rarest.

Capuchin monkeys are the ones with a prehensile tail. Best-known are the spider, squirrel, woolly and howler monkeys.

▶ *THE AMAZON RAIN FORESTS throb with life. The hot, moist atmosphere is ideal for plants. And the plants provide plenty of food for:*

- *agile monkeys;*
- *beautiful butterflies;*
- *slithering snakes;*
- *brightly colored tree frogs;*
- *squawking parrots;*
- *exquisite orchids.*

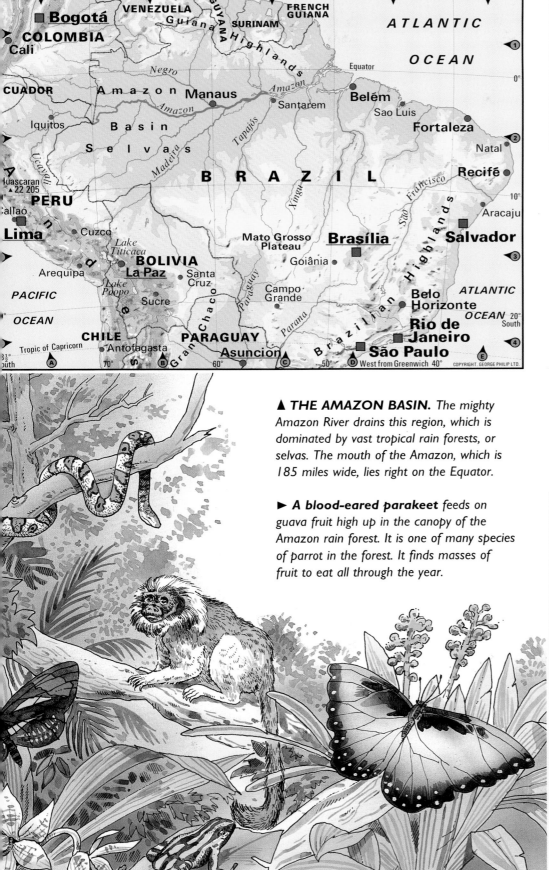

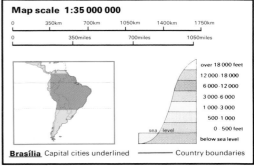

Map scale 1:35 000 000

| 0 | 350km | 700km | 1050km | 1400km | 1750km |

| 0 | 350 miles | 700 miles | 1050miles |

over 18 000 feet
12 000-18 000
6 000-12 000
3 000-6 000
1 000-3 000
500-1 000
sea level 0-500 feet
below sea level

Brasília Capital cities underlined ———— Country boundaries

TOOTHLESS TERMITE TASTERS

On the forest floor roam wild pigs, called peccaries, and tapirs. Tapirs are pony-sized animals that look a bit like a pig but are more closely related to the rhinoceros.

There are ants and termites by the billions in the forest leaf litter, providing rich pickings for the anteaters. These animals have no teeth and catch their prey with a long sticky tongue. The squirrel-size silky anteater and tamanduas stay largely in the trees. They have a prehensile tail to help them climb and for support. The 7-foot-long giant anteater is more of a ground creature, hunting mainly in the savanna.

The capybara, the world's biggest rodent, lives along the waterways. It looks like an oversize guinea pig, and its name means "master of the grass."

▲ **THE AMAZON BASIN.** The mighty Amazon River drains this region, which is dominated by vast tropical rain forests, or selvas. The mouth of the Amazon, which is 185 miles wide, lies right on the Equator.

▶ **A blood-eared parakeet** feeds on guava fruit high up in the canopy of the Amazon rain forest. It is one of many species of parrot in the forest. It finds masses of fruit to eat all through the year.

Temperate South America

The huge temperate zone in South America begins south of the Tropic of Capricorn. The main geographic regions east of the Andes are the Gran Chaco, the pampas, and the Patagonian Plateau.

Much of the Gran Chaco is arid, with thorny scrub and low hardwood forest. To the east are the rolling Brazilian Highlands, where the Parana River rises. Here grow extensive softwood forests of Parana pine.

In the south the Gran Chaco leads into the pampas. It is a vast grassland region that provides rich grazing for wildlife and for domesticated livestock.

GETTING COOLER

South of the pampas the land rises to the Patagonian Plateau. The soil is poorer here, the climate cool and dry, and the vegetation sparse. On the wetter western side of the southern Andes, however, there is thick forest. It is largely of Chilean pine, often called the monkey puzzle tree and grown in gardens in North America and Europe.

▲ *A copper-rumped hummingbird* hovers near a brightly colored flower, wings whirring rapidly. It is about to plunge in its long bill to sip the sweet nectar inside. It is one of hundreds of hummingbird species found in the region.

▲ *This armadillo* has nine bands of "armor plate" on its body. It is the common, or long-nosed, armadillo, which is found in all habitats in the region except the driest deserts and the highest mountains.

◀ *A black-browed albatross* and chick in their neat nest. Albatrosses raise only one young at a time. They breed mainly on the southwest coast but spend most of the year gliding across the southern oceans.

FE IN THE SCRUB

ran Chaco, which means "hunting land," has teresting wildlife. Among the many animal nters are cats like the puma, jaguar, and celot. A very rare wolf, the maned wolf, is other predator. It has a reddish coat d very long legs. It feeds on rabbits, small dents, and even armadillos. Armadillos can ten foil their enemies, however, by rolling into a tight ball. Their "armor-plated" ck then protects them. Biggest of all is the nt armadillo, up to 5 feet long.

Armadillos also inhabit the pampas. So do inea pigs, or cavies, and other cavy-like dents. Among them are the rat-like tuco-co and the much bigger mara. The mara s long legs and looks rather like a small er. The coypu, or nutria, is a large rodent at prefers a watery habitat, living along vers and lakes. With webbed hind feet, it is excellent swimmer.

THE GRASS-COVERED PAMPAS

the "prairie" of South America. The Gran aco region to the north is partly forested rubland. In the south the climate is cool; tends to be wet in the west near the Pacific d dry in the east by the Atlantic Ocean.

▼ *In a beech forest* in southern Chile, a spider waits in the center of its web for a meal to come its way. It has woven in a thicker zigzag thread, which makes the web more easily seen, and avoided, by birds which would destroy it if they flew into it.

GRASSLANDS GRAZERS

The most common grazers of the pampas are the guanaco and the rhea. The guanaco is one of the camel-like lamoids (see page 71). The rhea is a flightless bird rather like an ostrich, but smaller.

LIVELY WATERS

The coasts and waters around the southern part of the continent are alive with seabirds, such as petrels, shearwaters, albatrosses and gulls, and penguins.

There are also great colonies of penguins and seabirds on the Falkland Islands and South Georgia. These islands are havens for such wildlife because they have no large predators. South American sea lions, fur seals, and elephant seals breed there too. The male southern elephant seal is a massive beast. It is nearly 16 feet long and weighs over 2 tons!

▼ *A southern right whale* thrusts its 50-ton body from the water. This whale winters around the coasts of the region, but it spends the summer feeding in the plankton-rich waters of the somewhat colder Antarctic Ocean (see pages 76 and 77).

Map scale 1:35 000 000

| 0 | 350km | 700km | 1050km |
| 0 | 350miles | | 700miles |

——— Country boundaries
Santiago Capital cities underlined

over 18 000 feet
12 000 - 18 000
6 000 - 12 000
3 000 - 6 000
1 000 - 3 000
500 - 1 000
0 - 500 feet
below sea level

Polar Regions

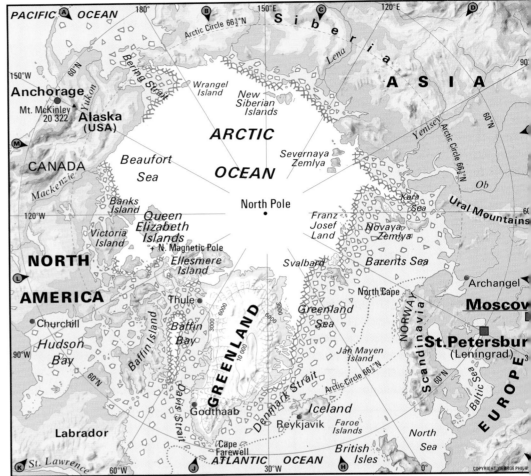

Among the worst places on Earth for living things are the polar regions. There the temperature remains very low throughout the year. In winter, it can fall to more than −76°F. Strangely, the polar regions have little rain or snowfall. They are as dry as some of the hottest deserts.

The polar region in the northern hemisphere is called the Arctic. There is no land here, just the Arctic Ocean. Because it is so cold, the ocean is covered with thick ice. The polar region in the southern hemisphere is called the Antarctic. The landmass of Antarctica occupies most of it. In certain places the ice is over 2.5 miles thick!

WHITE HUNTERS

Some living things are able to survive in the polar regions. In the Arctic the polar bear is king. It lives mainly on the ice, hunting seals for food. Its coat is very thick, which helps protect it from the cold. A layer of fat beneath the skin gives added protection.

A much smaller predator, the arctic fox, often follows polar bears to feed on the remains of their kills. But it usually stays on land, on the tundra region around the Arctic Ocean. There it hunts other creatures, including the arctic hare.

▲ **Cool customer.** This is in northern Alaska, where the temperature is well below freezing. But this harbor, or common, seal is not worried. The thick layer of fat, or blubber, beneath its skin keeps out the bitter cold.

▲ **Polar bears** roam the Arctic tundra and also hunt on the floating pack ice in the Arctic Ocean. Their white coat gives them good camouflage on the snowy wastes when they are stalking their prey, usually seals.

▲ **THE NORTH POLE** is located in the middle of the Arctic Ocean. Most of this ocean is frozen the whole year round, forming what is called the northern polar ice cap. The treeless land, or tundra, to the south of the ocean in North America, Europe, and Asia is also snow-covered for many months. In summer it becomes the breeding ground for many species of geese, swans, and other birds, as well as hordes of insects.

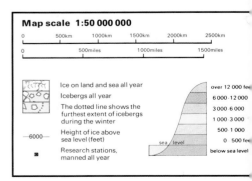

Map scale 1:50 000 000

Ice on land and sea all year	over 12 000 feet
Icebergs all year	6 000–12 000
The dotted line shows the furthest extent of icebergs during the winter	3 000–6 000
	1 000–3 000
Height of ice above sea level (feet)	500–1 000
Research stations, manned all year	0–500 below sea level

STREAMLINED SEALS

Polar bears feed mainly on ringed seals. But they also eat bearded and harp seals. These seals abound in Arctic waters. Their sleek, streamlined bodies make them swift swimmers. Several kinds of fur seals live in these waters too, as do the huge walruses. They can tip the scales at over 1 ton.

Walruses are not found in south polar regions, but seals are. They include the Weddell, southern elephant and crabeater seals. There are more crabeaters in the world than any other kind of seal.

CHOPPING WHALES

Whales appear in both Arctic and Antarctic waters, mainly during the summer. They feed on the plankton and small crustaceans that thrive there. In the fall most species migrate south from the Arctic or north from the

Antarctic to breed in warmer waters. The gray whale, for example, migrates from the Arctic to Baja California in winter. Narwhals and bowheads are mainly Arctic species. The huge sperm, blue and humpback whales can be seen in both Arctic and Antarctic waters.

PENGUIN CAPERS

The best-known creatures in Antarctica are the penguins. These birds cannot fly, but they are especially skillful swimmers. Their wings have turned into flippers to propel them swiftly through the water. They feed on fish and crustaceans in the sea but come ashore to breed. The commonest species is the Adélie penguin, while the largest is the emperor. The emperor male incubates the single egg, holding it on its feet and keeping it warm under a flap of skin.

THE SOUTH POLE is located on land, in the middle of the deep-frozen continent Antarctica. Here there is hardly any tundra. Only a narrow strip of land around the edge becomes ice-free in summer.

► *Looking immaculate* in its sleek plumage, an emperor penguin braves the Antarctic cold. The emperor is the biggest of the 16 species of penguin, growing up to 3 feet tall. It is the only one to breed in winter.

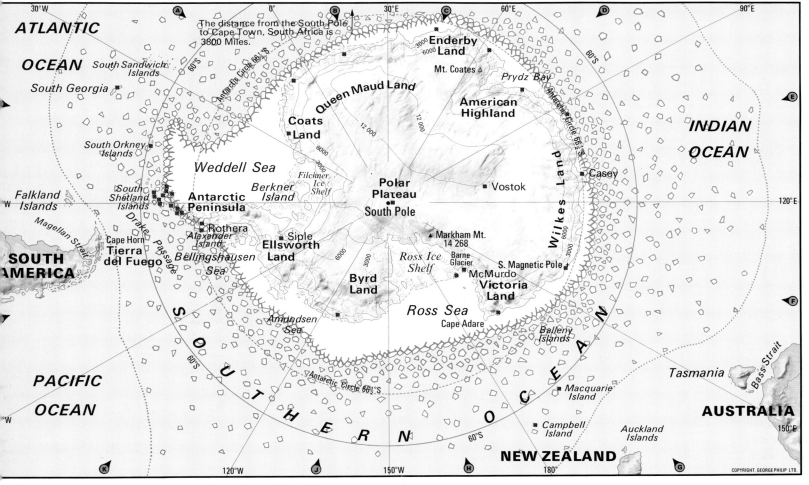

COPYRIGHT. GEORGE PHILIP LTD.

77

INDEX

Place names on maps

The first number given after each name is the page number; then a letter and another number tell you which square of the map you should look at. If a name goes through more than one square, the square given in the index is the one in which the biggest part of the name falls.

Names like Gulf of Mexico and Cape Horn are in the index as Mexico, Gulf of and Horn, Cape.

...t and animal index

...DLIFE MAPS – LISTS OF ANIMALS AND PLANTS

...ROPE page 24

33 Brambling
34 Eurasian river otter
35 Black stork
36 Harbour seal
37 Red squirrel
38 Roe deer
39 Grey heron
40 Mallard
41 European polecat
42 Grey partridge
43 Long-eared owl
44 Blue tit
45 Wild boar
46 European adder
47 Fallow deer
48 Greylag goose
49 European bison
50 Common buzzard
51 Hooded crow
52 Raven
53 Greater flamingo
54 Wild cat
55 Alpine marmot
56 Ibex
57 Chamois
58 Ring-necked pheasant
59 Eurasian badger
60 White spoonbill
61 Red fox
62 Common hamster
63 Golden eagle
64 Great cormorant
65 European hedgehog
66 Golden jackal
67 Great white pelican
68 Ground squirrel
69 Chestnut-bellied sandgrouse
70 European hare
71 Saiga
72 Great bustard
73 Eurasian bittern
74 Common egret
75 Red-footed falcon
76 Azure-winged magpie
77 Spanish goat
78 Lynx
79 Red falcon
80 Barbary ape
81 Mouflon
82 White stork
83 European coot
84 Bonelli's eagle
85 Sand boa
86 Griffon vulture
87 Greek tortoise
88 Wild goat
89 Pallid harrier
90 Urial
91 Anatolian leopard
92 Narwhal
93 Herring
94 Harbour porpoise
95 Atlantic cod
96 Right whale
97 Bluefin (tuna)

ASIA page 33
1 Walrus
2 Polar bear
3 Fur seal
4 Snowy owl
5 Siberian ibex
6 Sable
7 Red squirrel
8 Argalis
9 Sea otter
10 Ural owl
11 European polecat
12 Eurasian river otter
13 Kolinsky
14 Alpine marmot
15 Moose
16 Manchurian tiger
17 Wapiti
18 Leopard
19 Eurasian badger
20 Japanese giant salamander
21 Bobak
22 Snow leopard
23 Père David's deer
24 Manchurian hare
25 Arctic fox
26 Roe deer
27 Ringed seal
28 Russian desman
29 Asiatic ass
30 Musk deer
31 Asian black bear
32 Przewalski's horse
33 Blue sheep
34 Jerboa
35 Brown eared pheasant
36 Raccoon dog
37 Jay
38 Antelope
39 Jungle cat
40 Caracal
41 Jackal
42 Rock dove
43 Onager/Asiatic ass
44 Northern tiger (possible area)
45 Porcupine
46 Ground jay
47 Hyena
48 Woolly hare
49 West Asian dhole
50 Himalayan tahr
51 Thorold's deer
52 Chital
53 Kiang (Asiatic ass)
54 Chiru
55 Yak
56 Golden snub-nosed monkey
57 Giant panda
58 Large Indian civet
59 Red panda
60 Chinese softshell turtle
61 Red-billed blue magpie
62 Sambar
63 Masked palm civet
64 Silver pheasant
65 Flying gecko
66 Nubian goat
67 Hamadryas baboon
68 Spiny-tailed lizard
69 Glider (no longer present?)
70 Sloth bear
71 Gharial
72 Goral
73 Blackbuck
74 Crab-eating mongoose
75 Satyr tragopan
76 Banded mongoose
77 Sureli
78 Indian rhinoceros
79 Takin
80 Malayan tapir
81 Indian elephant
82 Indian python
83 Leopard cat
84 Indian tiger
85 Chinese pangolin
86 Slow loris
87 Yak
88 Hoolock gibbon
89 Gaur
90 Asian cobra
91 Clouded leopard
92 Serow
93 Greater moonrat
94 Philippine colugo
95 Green turtle
96 Indian star tortoise
97 Indian (black) vulture
98 Cheetah
99 Indian muntjac
100 Red-billed blue magpie
101 Toque macaque
102 Large Indian civet
103 Nilgai
104 Great hornbill
105 Hill mynah
106 Indian wild boar
107 Hawksbill turtle
108 Slender loris
109 Sureli
110 Tree shrew
111 Rhinoceros
112 Common palm civet
113 Great argus pheasant
114 Butterfly lizard
115 Asiatic brush-tailed porcupine
116 Lesser mouse deer
117 Sun bear
118 Wreathed hornbill
119 Estuarine crocodile
120 Teledu
121 Bowerbird
122 Malaysian civet
123 Crab-eating macaque
124 Colubrid snake
125 Crested porcupine
126 Marbled eel
127 Siamang
128 Flying dragon
129 Otter civet
130 Proboscis monkey
131 Orang-utan
132 Babirusa
133 Moor macaque
134 Moluccan cockatoo
135 Banded linsang
136 Sail-fin lizard
137 Moloch gibbon
138 Oriental water snake
139 Black giant squirrel
140 Ebony leaf monkey
141 Flying fox
142 Spotted cuscus
143 Rusa deer
144 Narwhal
145 Beluga
146 Striped marlin
147 Japanese saw-shark
148 Pearl oyster
149 Wolf herring
150 Sperm whale
151 Swordfish
152 Ganges dolphin
153 Minke whale
154 Dugong
155 Dugong

AFRICA page 45
1 Horned viper
2 Edmi
3 Golden jackal
4 Great white pelican
5 African chameleon
6 Dorcas gazelle
7 Egyptian mongoose
8 Sacred ibis
9 Desert jerboa
10 Fennec fox
11 Caracal or African lynx
12 Barbary macaque
13 Spotted hyena
14 Gerbil
15 Senegalese lion
16 Ruppel's vulture
17 Greater flamingo
18 Gemsbok
19 Sidestriped jackal
20 Beisa oryx
21 Saddle-bill stork
22 Giraffe
23 Nile crocodile
24 Secretary bird
25 Patas monkey
26 Diana monkey
27 Aardvark
28 Common eland
29 Pygmy hippopotamus
30 Black colobus monkey
31 Mandrill
32 North African ostrich
33 African leopard
34 African starling
35 African elephant
36 Marabou stork
37 Whale-headed stork
38 Honey badger
39 Hamadryas baboon
40 Gerenuk
41 African ass
42 African cheetah
43 Addax
44 Hippopotamus
45 Bongo
46 Antelope
47 African forest buffalo
48 Warthog
49 African gray parrot
50 Okapi
51 Congo peacock
52 Chimpanzee
53 Gorilla
54 Lion
55 Roan antelope
56 White-tailed gnu
57 Cape buffalo
58 Hawk eagle
59 Sable antelope
60 African starling
61 Maxwell's duiker
62 Serval
63 Black rhinoceros
64 Egyptian vulture
65 Guereza
66 Green turtle
67 Rock python
68 Black crowned crane
69 Turaco
70 Macaroni penguin
71 Cape fur seal
72 Greater kudu
73 Cape hyrax
74 Springbok
75 Chapman's zebra
76 White rhinoceros
77 Aardwolf
78 Klipspringer
79 Bontebok
80 Puff adder
81 Ruffed lemur
82 Brown lemur
83 Cuckoo-shrike
84 Fossa
85 Ring-tailed lemur
86 Lesser spotted dogfish
87 Common dolphin
88 Skate
89 Great white shark
90 Killer whale
91 Sooty albatross
92 Sperm whale
93 Hammerhead shark
94 Flying fish
95 Puffer fish

AUSTRALIA page 54
1 Mangrove plant
2 Coconut palm
3 Pandanus tree
4 Pincushion tree
5 Australian kingia tree
6 Wattle tree
7 Saltbush
8 Triodia bush
9 Macrozamia pine
10 Araucaria pine
11, 12, 13 Eucalyptus trees
14 Brachychiton tree
15, 16 Eucalyptus trees
17 Nothofagus shrub
18 Podocarpus tree
19 Australian water rat
20 Bird of paradise
21 Short-beaked echidna
22 Spotted cuscus
23 Spotted cuscus
24 Common palm civet
25 Estuarine crocodile
26 Common asiatic monitor
27 Phascogale
28 Red kangaroo
29 Pheasant
30 Wallaby
31 Green turtle
32 Short-beaked echidna
33 Vulture
34 Common brushtail possum
35 Rat
36 Duck-billed platypus
37 Hawksbill turtle
38 Honey possum
39 European rabbit
40 Brush-tailed bettong
41 Greater rabbit-eared bandicoot
42 Black swan
43 Numbat
44 Moloch
45 Dingo
46 Spiny-cheeked honeyeater
47 Phascogale
48 Eastern grey kangaroo
49 Emu
50 Kultar
51 Black cockatoo
52 Koala
53 Laughing kookaburra
54 Sugar glider
55 Brush-tailed rock wallaby
56 Eastern quoll
57 Superb lyrebird
58 Thylacine wolf
59 Tasmanian devil
60 Short-beaked echidna
61 Tuatara
62 Huia
63 Parrot
64 Short-tailed bat
65 Maori rat
66 Brown kiwi
67 Penguin
68 Tui
69 Pygmy right whale
70 Marlin
71 Dugong
72 Eastern grey kangaroo
73 Ducked-billed platypus
74 Sugar glider
75 Emu
76 Eastern quoll
77 Koala
78 Brush-tailed rock wallaby
79 Antipodean goose
80 Thylacine wolf
81 Snoek
82 Port Jackson shark
83 Sei whale
84 Tuatara
85 Crest fish
86 Brown kiwi
87 Fiordland penguin
88 Risso's dolphin
89 Tui

OCEANIA page 57
1 Coconut palm
2 Metroxylon palm
3 Banana tree
4 Macrozamia pine
5 Pandanus tree
6 Wattle tree
7 Acacia tree
8 Australian kingia tree
9 Araucaria pine
10 Nothofagus shrub
11 Seed fern
12 Kentia palm
13 Saltbush
14 Triodia bush
15 Brachychiton tree
16 Eucalyptus tree
17 Eucalyptus tree
18 Podocarpus tree
19 Kauri pine
20 Lorikeet
21 Polynesian gecko
22 Scrub fowl
23 Ascension Island frigate bird
24 False killer whale
25 Tiger shark
26 Green turtle
27 Stony coral
28 Clownfish
29 Dugong
30 Rabbitfish
31 Hermit crab
32 Kauai akioloa
33 Wilson's storm petrel
34 Bottle-nosed dolphin
35 Brown noddy
36 Wandering albatross
37 Tiger cat
38 Eclectus parrot
39 Papuan bat
40 Australian snake-necked turtle
41 Cassowary
42 Australian water rat
43 Tree kangaroo
44 Bird of paradise
45 Wallaby
46 Short-beaked echidna
47 Spotted cuscus
48 Fruit bat
49 Sacred kingfisher
50 Woodford's bat
51 Lorikeet
52 Koala
53 Common echidna
54 Common brushtail possum
55 Barracuda
56 Hawksbill turtle
57 Kagu
58 Great crested grebe
59 Cockatoo
60 Green parrot
61 Shrike
62 Mynah bird
63 Stingray
64 White tern
65 Flying fox
66 Wilson's storm petrel
67 Moray eel
68 Moray eel
69 Blue lory
70 Sea turtle
71 Purple-capped lory
72 Eastern grey kangaroo
73 Ducked-billed platypus
74 Sugar glider
75 Emu
76 Eastern quoll
77 Koala
78 Brush-tailed rock wallaby
79 Antipodean goose
80 Thylacine wolf
81 Snoek
82 Port Jackson shark
83 Sei whale
84 Tuatara
85 Crest fish
86 Brown kiwi
87 Fiordland penguin
88 Risso's dolphin
89 Tui

NORTH AMERICA page 59
1 Alaskan fur seal
2 Grizzly bear
3 Moose
4 Thinhorn sheep
5 Surf scoter
6 Snow goose
7 Glaucous gull
8 Tundra wolf
9 Common eider
10 Caribou
11 Parasitic jaeger
12 Harp seal
13 Polar bear
14 Willow ptarmigan
15 Black guillemot
16 Gyrfalcon
17 Snowshoe hare
18 Great black-backed gull
19 Artic lemming
20 Snowy owl
21 Musk ox
22 Walrus
23 American black bear
24 Great cormorant
25 Grey wolf
26 American bison
27 Wapiti
28 Whooper swan
29 Northern lynx
30 Northern gannet
31 Grizzly bear
32 Bald eagle
33 American badger
34 Common raccoon
35 Mallard
36 Wolverine
37 Sea otter
38 Mountain goat
39 Coyote
40 Steller sea lion
41 Pronghorn
42 Spotted owl
43 Hellbender
44 Prairie chicken
45 Prairie dog
46 Black-footed ferret
47 North American beaver
48 Virginia opossum
49 American mink
50 Osprey
51 Grey squirrel
52 White-tailed deer
53 Elegant tern
54 King snake
55 Collared peccary
56 Northern oriole
57 American alligator
58 Grey fox
59 Striped skunk
60 Wild turkey
61 Ocelot
62 Flying squirrel
63 Painted turtle
64 American crocodile
65 American bullfrog
66 Timber or Banded rattlesnake
67 Vulture
68 Mexican beaded lizard
69 Quetzal
70 Yapok
71 Harpy eagle
72 Curassow
73 Greater flamingo
74 Paca
75 Hawksbill turtle
76 Narwhal
77 Bowhead whale
78 Common mackerel
79 Atlantic cod
80 Atlantic salmon
81 Barracuda
82 Cichlid
83 Swordfish
84 Parrotfish
85 Flying fish
86 Tiger shark
87 Common dolphin
88 Sperm whale

SOUTH AMERICA page 68
1 Hawksbill turtle
2 Oilbird
3 American crocodile
4 Spectacled bear
5 Humboldt's woolly monkey
6 Pale-throated three-toed sloth
7 South American river turtle
8 Ocelot
9 Squirrel monkey
10 West Indian manatee
11 Common tegu
12 Bushmaster
13 Hyacinth macaw
14 Giant armadillo
15 South American knife-fish
16 White faced capuchin
17 Harpy eagle
18 Toco toucan
19 Puffed parrot
20 Prehensile-tailed porcupine
21 Linne's two-toed sloth
22 Crab-eating raccoon
23 Red howler
24 Brazilian tapir
25 Ring-tailed coati
26 White-tailed deer
27 Mountain tapir
28 Black caiman
29 Greek anaconda
30 False vampire bat
31 Amazon dolphin
32 Kinkajou
33 Agouti
34 Oriole
35 Giant otter
36 Arapaima
37 Military macaw
38 Capybara
39 Toucan
40 Great kiskadee
41 Green turtle
42 Turkey vulture
43 Mountain viscacha
44 Brown-headed cowbird
45 Vicuña
46 King vulture
47 Little red brocket
48 Tabulated tortoise
49 White-lipped peccary
50 Crab-eating fox
51 Marsh deer
52 Puma
53 Common marmoset
54 Yellow armadillo
55 Jaguarundi
56 Fairy hummingbird
57 Hog-nosed skunk
58 Jaguar
59 Coati
60 Boa constrictor
61 Chinchilla
62 Least seed snipe
63 Azara's fox
64 Paraguayan or South anaconda
65 Tayra
66 Broad-nosed caiman
67 Southern tamandua
68 Common vampire bat
69 Coypu
70 Paca
71 Caracara
72 Andean condor
73 Puma
74 Maned wolf
75 Common long-nosed armadillo
76 Pampas deer
77 Red-winged tinamou
78 Giant anteater
79 Grison
80 Black howler
81 Steamer duck
82 Guanaco
83 Viscacha
84 Otter turtle
85 New World martin
86 Grey rhea
87 Southern pudu
88 Mara or Patagonian cavy
89 Black-necked swan
90 Harrier hawk
91 Macaroni penguin
92 Snowy sheathbill
93 South American sea lion
94 Galapagos giant tortoise
95 Marine iguana
96 Galapagos land iguana
97 Hammerhead shark
98 Barracuda
99 Cowfish
100 Dory
101 Lesser electric ray
102 Whale shark
103 Fin whale
104 Common dolphin
105 Sperm whale

Photo credits
t=top, b=bottom, l=left, r=right, c=center

A = Aquila, PW = Premaphotos Wildlife:
KGPM = K.G. Preston-Mafham, RAPM = R.A. Preston-Mafham.

4l,r KGPM/PW. 5l KGPM/PW. 5r Mike Wilkes/A/PW. 6 KGPM/PW. 8l RAPM/PW. 8r, 9l & r KGPM/PW. 11t K. Ghani/PW. 11l Wayne Lankinen/A/PW. 11c KGPM/PW. 11r Wayne Lankinen/A/PW. 13t,c,bl,bc,br KGPM/PW. 14l,c,r KGPM/PW. 15l,c,r KGPM/PW. 16tl,bl KGPM/PW. 16r Jeff Foott/Survival Anglia. 19tl,tr,bl,br KGPM/PW. 20 KGPM/PW. 21 Mike Wilkes/A/PW. 22 M. Birkhead/A/PW. 23tl KGPM/PW. 23tr C & T Stuart/A/PW. 23bl Richard T. Mills/A/PW. 23br M. Birkhead/A/PW. 25l Robert Maier/A/PW. 25r KGPM/PW. 25b Robert Maier/A/PW. 26t M. Preston-Mafham/PW. 26bl RAPM/PW. 26br KGPM/PW. 29t

RAPM/PW. 29cl Robert Maier/A/PW. 29cr N.W.Harwood/A/PW. 29b RAPM/PW. 30 R. Siegal/A/PW. 31l A.J.Bond/A/PW. 31r Siegal/A/PW. 32t KGPM/PW. 32bl,br K.Ghani/PW. 35 Joanna Van Gruisen/Survival Anglia. 36, 37t,bl KGPM/PW. 37br Lee Lyon/Survival Anglia. 38 K.Ghani/A/PW. 39 Brian Hawkes/A/PW. 40t G.D. Plage/Survival Anglia. 40b N. Jagannathan/A/PW. 41 D. & M. Plage/Survival Anglia. 42l,r,43 KGPM/PW. 44tl,tr,b KGPM/PW. 46t H & J. Erisksen/Birkhead/A/PW. 46b,47,48 KGPM/PW. 49t M. Birkhead/A/PW. 49c,b KGPM/PW. 50 KGPM/PW. 51l John Stidworthy. 51b KGPM/PW. 52tl,tr,b KGPM/PW. 55t,b KGPM/PW. 56t,bl,br KGPM/PW. 58t Wayne Lankinen/A/PW. 58bl KGPM/PW. 58br M.C. Wilkes/A/PW. 61tl,tr Wayne Lankinen/A/PW. 61b Edgar T. Jones/A/PW. 62t KGPM/PW. 62bl Wayne Lankinen/A/PW. 62br KGPM/PW. 63, 64t Wayne Lankinen/A/PW. 64b M. Wilkes/A/PW. 65 Jeff Foott/Survival Anglia. 66 KGPM/PW. 67 B. Hawkes/A/PW. 69, 70, 71, 72, 73 KGPM/PW. 74t J.J. Brooks/A/PW. 75b D. & J. Bartlett/Survival Anglia. 76l Joel Bennett/Survival Anglia. 76r Wayne Lankinen/A/PW. 77 R. Gill/A/PW.